River of Fire

The Rattlesnake Fire and the Mission Boys

John N. Maclean

Ridgetop dozer line runs to this point

Newer fire break

Gillespy Ranch

Initial fire spread ran from near the road at Oleta Point uphill toward what's now a fire break.

Oleta Point

Memorial Overlook

Missionary Rock

Lafferty ran up the ridge, then downhill here to warn the boys.

Missionary Spot Fire (and lunch spot)

This is the recovery road, not the original line of the fire.

Log chute below the turn

Second spot fire

This dozer line runs uphill to a containment line in 1953

Powderhouse Turn

"High Point"

Today there is a little 2-track road along the top of the ridge. Up here somewhere was the little slopover where Vote and crew were working before recovering at Powderhouse Turn.

Dozer and hand line from Powderhouse Turn to High Point

Newer fire break

RIVER OF FIRE

The Rattlesnake Fire and the Mission Boys
COPYRIGHT © 2018 John N. Maclean

ALL RIGHTS RESERVED

An earlier version of this story was included in the book
Fire and Ashes, published in 2003 by Henry Holt and Co.

Cover and interior photos by Kari Greer – kariphotos.com
Editing/design by AnderssonPublishing.com
Maps by John N. Maclean, Kari Greer and Kelly Andersson

Some discounts may be available on quantity purchases by
fire crews, associations, and others. Contact the author at
JohnMacleanBooks.com

ISBN: 978-0-692-07998-0
Printed in the United States of America

ALSO BY JOHN N. MACLEAN

FIRE ON THE MOUNTAIN
The True Story of the South Canyon Fire

FIRE AND ASHES
On the Front Lines of American Wildfire

THE THIRTYMILE FIRE
A Chronicle of Bravery and Betrayal

THE ESPERANZA FIRE
Arson, Murder, and the Agony of Engine 57

DEDICATION
To Kelly Andersson, my longtime backstop

Photos & Maps:

INTRODUCTION

It was evening, about 10 p.m., when the wind over a brush-choked canyon in northern California's Glenn County unexpectedly shifted and began to roar downhill. A fire had been burning since midday on the upper reaches of the canyon on the Mendocino National Forest, a bit over 100 miles north of Sacramento. The fresh, violent wind picked up embers from the fire and spun them down into the depths of the canyon, where the embers transformed into a thunderous torrent of fire, as though a dam had burst.

The sight mesmerized veteran firefighters. Long, fatal minutes passed before they remembered a crew of twenty-four men stationed in the canyon below. The crew had hunkered down in a ravine to eat supper and had posted no lookouts.

The alarm was raised, but it was late. Fifteen of the men in the lower crew began a race with fire down the canyon while another nine scrambled upward to safety. Other firefighters watched in horror from canyon slopes as the torrent of fire hurtled toward the fifteen men and snuffed their headlamps, one after another.

The loss of fifteen firefighters on the Rattlesnake Fire, which occurred July 9, 1953, stood unmatched for many years, but it sparked a nationwide program to deliberately burn chaparral and reduce the risk of uncontrolled fire. The program, though, was severely curtailed under a series of environmental challenges beginning in the 1970s.

1

The Rattlesnake Fire helped inspire rules for wildfire safety that remain in force today. The Forest Service, conscience-struck by a mounting death toll from this and other fires, assembled a task force in 1957 that produced the Ten Standard Fire Orders, the bedrock of firefighter safety, and the number of multiple-fatality fires dropped dramatically after 1957.

The fire also provided a lesson about the limits of punishment for arson. Stan Pattan, the son of a prominent Forest Service engineer, confessed to setting the Rattlesnake Fire so he could get a job on the fire crew. He was taken into custody while working as a cook at the fire camp. Pattan served three years of a possible twenty-year sentence in San Quentin but he dodged murder charges and a more severe sentence because he had not intended to harm anyone. He returned home, where he worked many years as a wildlife artist and had no further trouble with the law.

The spring after the Rattlesnake Fire, two young Forest Service men, dismayed by the loss of life, took drip torches and on their own authority ignited a huge swath of chaparral near the site of the fire. Deliberate burning, they believed, would have prevented the deaths on the Rattlesnake Fire.

The Forest Service, to its credit, didn't discipline them but instead made the burn a model for the region.

"Hopefully, there is some solace in the fact that this tragedy woke up the Forest Service and other firefighting agencies," Dan Chisholm, supervisor of the Mendocino National Forest, said at a 1993 memorial dedication near the fire site.

But fire remains a brutal teacher. The ongoing losses of firefighters underscore the truth that fire ultimately eludes human control. The effects of fatal fires linger like heavy smoke for those who knew and loved those who fell. Hope lies in sifting the ashes to learn a lesson, no matter how imperfectly.

~ From an op-ed by John N. Maclean
published in the *Los Angeles Times,* October 2013

FOREWORD – PASSING IT ON

Don Will, May 2018

RATTLESNAKE CANYON IS A SPECIAL PLACE to me. I find a strange sense of peace and tranquility every time I go there. Each spring I hook up my 23-foot travel trailer and head to Long Point and set up there for a couple of days. It's a nice flat ridge with a view off to the east, looking down on Powderhouse Turn.

I go there each year to reflect and remember. Remember young men who perished there. I consider it one of my duties, to remember and to be a conduit of the past, to keep their sacrifice alive.

View from the site of the old Long Point Lookout

While there I start each day with a slow drive down Forest Road 7, past the memorial the USFS put up on the new Highway 7, which leads one to look out over Grindstone Canyon. It's a misleading memorial, on the ridge that divides Rattlesnake Canyon and Grindstone Canyon. It's an error we corrected back in 1993 when the Mendocino Hotshots packed a big wooden cross into Rattlesnake under the cover of night and set it at the site where the Missionary boys perished.

I always park at Powderhouse Turn, and there I take a few moments to breathe the air, feel the wind, smell the spring chaparral.

I think of Charlie Lafferty, who was a family friend of my uncle, Gil Ward. He worked with Charlie and they were lifelong friends. Uncle Gil told me that he and Charlie used to drive up Forest Road 7 and burn out the turnouts in the spring, so that hunters stopping to smoke there wouldn't start a fire. I think often of Charlie and the remorse he carried for the rest of his days.

I always walk down to the site of the spot fire and sit. It's very pleasant there on a spring morning. Birds are flittering around, wildflowers are blooming, and the chaparral has a green-up fragrance. I sit right where the Missionaries sat and had their lunch that fateful night in 1953. I imagine I can hear their voices, hear their crew banter, hear their pre-meal prayer.

I continue on then, up the escape trail they took when Charlie made his gallant run to warn them to run downhill, away from the fire. I reach the first cross, then the next. I think of what they were feeling as the fire was chasing and overtaking them. I think of those young men in the prime of life clawing their way through the thick chaparral at night. I reach the small ridge where Stanley Vote broke away and bulled his way straight uphill trying in vain to reach the top of Powderhouse ridge, and safety. I always climb to his cross and let him know we remember.

I slide my way back down to the recovery road, the road that was cut in by dozer. They backed in stake side trucks on that dozer line, to load up fifteen fatalities. I stop at the Mendocino Hotshot cross, the largest cross in the canyon, and remember the night we packed it in and set it. That cross stood as a Hotshot Secret for years, only to make many wonder where it had come from, how did it get there. We knew. And we were proud of it.

I walk past the big cross and down to the small swale where Bob Powers and eight others perished. I always let Bob and the others know we remember. I usually sit there for a while, and think of what they saw, and when they realized they had only minutes or seconds to live. I think of their families, their sorrow, the fear, the bravery, the sacrifice.

And finally, I take the long walk down to Cecil Hitchcock, the young man who was so close to safety, who almost made it out the bottom, only to get hung up on berry bushes and then overrun by the fire. I usually sit there for the longest time. He is alone, all by himself in the bottom of that canyon. It's there I have my lunch, and a drink of cool water. I find myself having a conversation with young Cecil. I tell him it's me again, and another year has gone by. Last year I left my Team 4 hat with him, and I'd like to think he appreciated that.

I end my day back at Powderhouse Turn, the ICP for the fire. If I sit and really listen, I can hear the dozers coming down from High Point, I can hear Charlie and the others talking about tactics, and I can feel Charlie's pain after he made it back here after his run to warn the Missionaries.

I open the tailgate of my truck and sit there, cooling down and wiping sweat off my face. I think of fire behavior, fuel moisture, local winds. It all comes together for me, there on the tailgate of my truck. I think of the tragedy and of the memorial that Jim Barry, Daren Dalrymple, Jon Tishner, and others finally made a reality. A fine overlook here in the canyon, with the fifteen names and faces for all to see and honor. I'm glad we were the unofficial instigators of that official memorial, and I always smile when I think what power was born of a simple white cross that mysteriously appeared in 1993 – the power to move a federal agency to finally, officially, recognize these young men in the last canyon they walked in.

As I travel across the valley on my way back home, I always feel a sense of calm. I feel a sense that they have taught me the lesson, again. A lesson to pay attention to nature's ways when you're in her canyons. To always remember the events that led up to their deaths, to use this site as a learning platform, to honor them and remember them as teachers of our children.

In 2016 my son was hired on with a hotshot crew. He was so proud when he came home and told me he was on the crew, a crew where I had been a foreman for five years. He had spent his previous four summers working on a trail crew, running chainsaws and swinging a Pulaski building trails. He was a natural fit as a hotshot, a trait they recognized, and they were giving him a shot.

As a seventeen-year hotshot, I was proud of him for his achievement. I knew what attributes were required to even get a look from that crew. He had earned his own way onto the crew, and I was proud of him, but I was also experiencing another emotion – a father's emotion when your child is knowingly going into harm's way. I knew only too well the hazards and risks he would be exposed to. I knew it, but I told myself he would be working on a crew with long-standing overhead with extensive wildland experience. He would be on a crew with an outstanding safety record. He would be on a crew of good decision makers, fine leaders, hard workers with a tough PT program that demanded physical and mental excellence. They would accept nothing less.

So as a seventeen-year hotshot, I knew he was in good hands … but as a father, I wanted to be a part of those hands, and those hands were pointing me right back to Rattlesnake.

So, in late spring of 2016, a few weeks before his hotshot crew was starting up, we loaded up and headed out to Rattlesnake. I knew this father would find peace if I could open the son's ears and eyes and let Bob Powers, Stanley Vote, Cecil Hitchcock, and the other Missionaries sit him down and whisper their secrets to him. I just needed him to listen. I just needed to find peace.

We slowed at Oleta Point and I showed him where Stanford Pattan threw his match, then on to the Memorial Overlook. I explained the meaning of the memorial and we talked about the fifteen faces etched in the stone. I pointed out Bob's picture and told my son

Bob's story. I told him how Bob survived his time as a prisoner of war in WWII – only to die here in the canyon on the Rattlesnake Fire. I told him about Cecil's panicked and frantic run for survival that wouldn't last. I pointed out Stanley Vote's superhuman climb to safety that wouldn't be. We looked at the small white crosses that marked each location where a young man fell, and he asked why there was a large white cross set there in a rock outcrop. I told him that was Missionary Rock, and a group of hotshots had set that cross a long time ago, long before creation of the memorial to honor the fifteen. He was silent ... he was listening ... and he was looking ... and this father was smiling.

We drove around to Powderhouse turn. We parked there, climbed from the truck and walked to the edge of the canyon. We stood there looking down. I asked him to feel the upslope wind, a bit warm in the late spring. We broke off pieces of chaparral and smelled it, felt it, rolled it in our hands. We got on our hands and knees and talked about fuel loading, continuity, and physical characteristics of chaparral. I needed to walk him through the basic fuel, weather, and topographical influences on fire behavior. I needed Rattlesnake to be my own fire behavior laboratory for a day. I already had fifteen instructors here ready to present their lessons, and I was ready to have them start.

We walked down the recovery road to Missionary Rock. It's a short walk, but it's a walk that is worth a father taking his son on. As we dropped off below the top of the canyon, we felt the temperature change, and the breeze was blocked by the brush. It was easily five degrees warmer here, and the air was still. After a few minutes we were sweating and my son mentioned how much warmer it was here and how difficult it was to see anything.

As we walked, I stopped and stood straight with the brush as a backdrop. I asked him how tall he thought the brush was. He scrunched his face and guessed about ten feet.

I told him the last time Rattlesnake had burned was in 1988 and the brush we were now busting through was 28 years of growth. How high was the brush when the Missionaries were here? We tried to walk through it and it was difficult at best. I asked my son to think about and feel the adrenalin that Stanley Vote felt as he bulled his way straight up toward the ridge through brush that was taller and thicker – and at night with a fire chasing him. I asked him to remember that Stanley Vote had already worked all afternoon with his crew on the south side of the fire, before walking to High Point and then down to Powderhouse Turn where they asked for another assignment. The assignment that took them down into the canyon.

We walked to the spot fire, the one the Missionaries were sent to contain. We stood at the lunch spot and I asked him what he saw. He knew the answer; he didn't take long before he said he couldn't see anything. It was all tall brush and steep slopes. He asked why they were down there …

We talked about the access routes they used, no chainsaws, no brushed-out travel routes … they just turned on headlamps and busted their way in, into a tight narrow side drainage with a spot fire creeping around at mid-slope. The fifteen instructors said that

11

was just the way it was done in 1953. They asked is that how it's done now?

We walked out to Missionary Rock. We stood on the rock and looked at the topography. We pointed out the draws and drainages, we talked about the exposures and aspects, which ones heated first and cooled last. We talked about position on slope and where the Missionaries were when they were overrun. We talked the combination of chaparral and topography and the fire behavior that would result from that combination. My son said he thought it would not be too bad, the fire behavior, with that combination, and I had to agree.

Then the fifteen instructors whispered to me; they said it's time to talk about wind. They reminded me that wind changes everything. They reminded me that wind turns fires in directions that common sense says fire shouldn't go. Wind doesn't care if it's day or night, doesn't care if the brush is tall, short, thick or thin. Wind doesn't care if anyone is in the way.

I asked about adding wind, and he knew the answer. I asked him about adding wind at night, when temperatures are cooler, and humidity is higher. I asked him if he thought wind would be the missing puzzle that might dry the air, dry the fuels, and push a creeping surface fire up and into the tops of the brush. He could see that, he said. I asked him to add wind to the combination of fuels and topography and what the results might be. He looked thoughtfully around and then gestured into the air and replied that the fire could move up-slope into the drainages. I asked him what might change if the wind was blowing downslope.

He turned and looked down Powderhouse Canyon. He looked back at me and pointed. "There?"

I nodded. I asked him, "Look closer, look harder, and you may see young Cecil Hitchcock waving back."

I explained the events of the night of July 9, 1953 with wind added to the equation. I showed him the path the fire took when the wind decided to change everything. I showed him the group of nine crosses in the swale just downslope from the big cross and Missionary Rock. The last stand of Bob Powers and eight of the mission boys. I told him they were moving downhill to safety when the wind changed their fate.

As we walked back out of the canyon my son was silent and thoughtful. I could tell he'd had enough for one day, he had enough to think about. I knew he was putting the pieces together.

We climbed back up to the truck and sat there together on the tailgate cooling off and drinking water. I didn't want to push him, but I knew it was this father's duty to test the envelope. I reminded my son that firefighting is a game for keeps. It's a game with nature's rules that are time-tested and not negotiable. Luck is not part of the firefighting game, but skill and patience are. Applying knowledge and action will keep you out of harm's way. Understanding the combination of the factors we had studied all day is part of the skill. Identifying hazards and controlling risks are the keys. If it doesn't feel right, stop. Be patient, be skillful.

A small breeze came up and I heard the fifteen tell us there are a thousand Rattlesnake Canyons all across the nation and they all have their own secrets, secrets that they will tell those who take the time to listen.

My son jumped down off the tailgate, looked at me, and said two simple words. "Thanks, Dad." He said he'd learned a lot today and it made good sense. A simple sentence to most, but a wave of relief to me. I knew my instructors had done their job and my fire behavior laboratory had worked. I knew I'd found the peace I had come here looking for.

As we head for home, we pass by the Memorial overlook and we stop and get out, stand there for a minute. I look up on the hill and I'd like to think they are sitting there on Missionary Rock looking my way. I'd like to think they hear me when I tell them I'll see them again next spring, and I'd like to think they are smiling and waving back. I'd like to think they are saying they are looking forward to the next class. That's what I'd like to think ...

Postscript: The Rattlesnake Fire site has been a place of mourning, remembering, and paying respect to the fifteen who in 1953 gave everything they had as they ran to survive. It has been a place for firefighters to be quiet and to honor. It has been a place where lives ended, where family sorrows began. It has always been a sad place. A sad place where visitors would look at the crosses and then shake their heads as they drove away and say "too bad."

But now, after all these years, I can see Rattlesnake as a site of resurrection. A site of new beginnings. A site where young and old firefighters can come together and cherish the lessons the fifteen instructors are eagerly waiting to tell us about. They have a lesson that encourages firefighters to take a few minutes in their busy days and sit in the Rattlesnake classroom with them and hear their story. They are saying: Take this lesson and go forth and live. Live a long and productive life with your friends and family, and don't be sad for us any longer, but honor our memory by understanding what we did, why we did it, and the conditions and decisions that led us into this canyon.

(Don Will served as superintendent of the Mendocino Hotshots from 1988 to 1994.)

Don Will, Daren Dalrymple, Jon Tishner, Mendocino Hotshot Supes and Photo Support Team, take five at the lunch spot.

FOREWORD, DON WILL

THE ARSONIST – 2001

THE HOUSE IS SMALL, WHITE, AND TIDY, its porch screened by latticework. Trees shield it from the street. Far in the background, often in haze, are the brush-covered mountains of the Northern Coast Range. Just opposite the Lutheran Church on Main Street, the only residential street in the town of Artois, the house is in California's Central Valley about ninety miles north of Sacramento.

A few homes and businesses dot the highway a block from Main Street, but Artois has little to invite the occasional visitor, no franchise motels or restaurants, not even a major gas station. Artois (pronounced like "are toys") has few ties to the broader world, and that's one reason Stanford Philip Pattan chose to live there.

Pattan's house in Artois in 2001

17

The Pattan house has a large living room open to the kitchen and, off to one side, an art studio. In 2001 Pattan would rise at about five each morning and begin his daylong immersion in pencil sketches, tracings, oil paints, and canvases, creating realistic images of game animals, Indians, and landscapes. "I paint every feather of a bird, every hair of an animal," he told me; his artworks brought a modest supplement to his monthly Social Security check. On a wall of the studio was one of Pattan's proudest mementos, a snapshot of him standing next to Joe Montana, the legendary San Francisco 49ers quarterback. "He bought several of my paintings," Pattan said proudly, as though this confirmed a link to the larger world.

A self-proclaimed hermit, Pattan described his chosen life as "hibernation." Though frequently seen in town, he would not speak unless spoken to first. He used to hang paintings for sale on a wall of Nancy's Airport Café, a renowned gathering place in nearby Willows, where he would often go for a meal. One day at the café he overheard two young men discussing the artist whose paintings were on the wall.

"He's the guy who lit the Rattlesnake Fire," one said. Pattan recounted the moment with something like pride.

"He wasn't talking like it was a bad thing," he said. "When I got up to leave I took out one of my business cards and laid it on their table. 'You've been talking about me; I just thought you'd like to know I heard.'" He slipped away before they could react.

Pattan worked as a farmhand, an ambulance driver, and a well-regarded hunting and fishing guide. Retired and in his mid-seventies when I finally found him, almost a half-century after the Rattlesnake Fire, Pattan lived in his private world of artistic endeavor. Long hours at the easel helped diffuse the troubling memories of nearly fifty years before. A match flaring alongside a roadway in dry chaparral. Men and machines battling contrary and out-of-control canyon flames. The sickening moment of realization when he learned that his act of desperation, never intended to harm, had gone horribly, fatally wrong. And the lingering twilight world of remorse ever after.

Pattan was twenty-six at the time of the Rattlesnake Fire in 1953; in the years after that he lived a quiet, law-abiding life. His first wife, Portia Lee, with whom he had four children, divorced him while he was in prison. He married a second wife, Velda, after he was released but lost her to illness. In a bizarre but curiously fitting turn of fate, a third wife, Connie, lost her memory after she underwent surgery for a brain tumor. She woke up looking at a stranger, her husband, a man who had himself lived as a stranger to society for nearly fifty years. Connie and Stan Pattan divorced but became friends; she was a waitress at Nancy's Airport Café and came by the house just to say hello while I was there. She and Pattan spent a lot of time together.

> "He's the guy who lit the Rattlesnake Fire."

During the legal proceedings in the 1950s after the fire, Pattan refused all media requests for interviews. And after decades of silence, he was not easy to locate: his name was misspelled "Patton" in news and court documents, which sent researchers including me down a blind alley. Pattan told me that one writer, apparently no reporter, assumed that Pattan was dead – it was more than a decade after the fire – and wrote a newspaper story that described him in florid terms as a deliberate killer stalking the mountains looking for easy prey. A threatened lawsuit resulted in an out-of-court settlement, terms not disclosed.

Then one evening in 2001 his phone rang, intruding on his guarded existence.

I had been researching the 1953 Rattlesnake Fire and was consulting records in Willows, which is the headquarters of the Mendocino National Forest and also the Glenn County seat where county court records are stored. I had scoured the internet and asked around looking for "Patton" without success. Then sitting in my motel room in Willows one I night I remembered how I had started years before in the newspaper business and reached for the local telephone directory. I flipped it open to the first "P page" and there on the list was one Stanford Pattan.

It had to be the man; I picked up the phone.

It's difficult to know how to approach a man like Pattan, a near-recluse who had never spoken openly about a notorious criminal past. I had no plan, but when a man's voice answered the phone I said, in a moment of desperate improvisation, "I'm looking for the son of Philip Pattan."

The line was silent for a long moment. It must have been decades since anyone had struck that chord. Anyone researching Pattan, though, soon realizes that he had lived in the shadow of his father Philip, a well-respected Forest Service engineer. The younger Pattan was always being introduced as "Phil Pattan's boy," or "the son of Phil Pattan."

When the man on the other end of the phone answered my question, it was with audible pride.

"That's me," he said. I explained that I was doing research for a book and wanted to interview him about the Rattlesnake Fire. There was an even longer pause. Then Pattan replied, heavily, "All right. I'll talk to you about it."

FIFTEEN MINUTES LATER I DROVE UP to the house in Artois. The visit that followed is a marker in my years of association with Stan Pattan and the people of the Rattlesnake Fire.

The fire was fading from memory back then: the site where it happened was unmarked, isolated on a little-used side road, and dirty; time had taken its toll on those who had fought the fire, who were fewer in number each year. But since that visit the story of the fire has gained a new life, and its long-dead embers reach out now with renewed heat to touch lives and draw the past forward into the present, reclaiming the ground where it happened, reviving memory, uniting children with lost parents – one regained and lost again in a single day – and bringing families and old comrades together to honor their own.

The story also reaches into the future, to pass along life-saving lessons to new generations of firefighters. I am not the sole cause of the revival, but this story, first published in 2003, helped spark the process and stirred things up. One of the milestones in gathering and sharing the story came for me – because my heart was in my mouth when it happened – one soft fall evening in 2001 when I knocked on the door of the man who had lit the Rattlesnake Fire.

PATTAN ANSWERED THE DOOR standing a little hunched, as though defending against a body blow, but he did not cower. A man of medium but sturdy build, he gave the impression of suppressed physical power. His white hair was combed straight back.

He had strong facial features: a long face, heavily creased and marked by a prominent Roman nose, similar to a sketch he once made of a classic Indian face. I have that sketch still.

We were both a bit nervous at the outset of the encounter: I was wondering if I'd even be allowed inside the house. But Pattan was a man with a story to tell and I was someone who wanted to listen; he ushered me inside. It didn't take long to discover a shared interest that broke the ice: we both were avid fishermen and outdoorsmen. Another of his artworks that I have to this day is a handsome painting of King Salmon. We sat at a kitchen table with a red and white checked tablecloth, drank bad coffee from heavy mugs, and began to unravel the past. "You've got to understand," Pattan said, speaking like a man desperate to unburden himself of a great weight.

Pattan's life had not been a happy one, and he was eager to be seen as he saw himself, a sufferer at the hand of fate. The fire had been "more devastating to me than most people think it was," he said. Three of his and Portia Lee's four children – two boys and a girl – were killed in accidents on highways or, in the case of the oldest boy, by complications after surgery. The only happy notes in his life, it seemed, were the times he'd had a rod or a gun or a paintbrush in hand.

We had to start somewhere other than a long and overpowering list of miseries, so we began the interview with the odd spelling of the family name, which had confused me and others – it was regularly misspelled Patton in court records and media accounts. The Pattani family arrived in California from Italy with the California Gold Rush. They failed at mining, later took up farming, and somewhere along the line dropped the final letter from their name.

At the time of the Rattlesnake Fire, Pattan told me, he was overwhelmed by personal problems: heavy debts, inability to hold a job – and his pregnant wife, Portia Lee, had just left him to go back to her parents' home with their three children. A doctor later testified that Pattan was having migraine headaches every other day because of "worry and nervousness," what today might be diagnosed as depression or even PTSD.

Pattan had dropped out of high school to enlist in the navy. He had served as a cook aboard a Landing Ship, Tank (LST) during World War II and had participated in eight island invasions in the South Pacific, including the massive operations at Okinawa and Iwo Jima. The LSTs, affectionately nicknamed "large slow targets" or "large stationary targets," brought tanks, other vehicles, and supplies to assault beaches, and they often came under fire. Once when I visited him in later years he was watching an episode of *Baa Baa Blacksheep*, the television series about the squadron of misfits under Marine Corps aviator Greg "Pappy" Boyington and his World War II "Black Sheep Squadron" that became a terror in the Pacific theater. We sat silently and watched the show to its conclusion. "That was my war," Pattan said proudly.

Upon his return to civilian life after his navy stint, Pattan landed a job as a game warden with the U.S. Fish and Wildlife Service in the Tule Lake region of California, near the Oregon state line. He loved the outdoors and took to the job. "I was trained in law enforcement," he says with intended irony. But his wife, Portia Lee, could not stand the isolation of the area and forced a move back to Willows, where the family fell on hard times.

Pattan was always good for a hunting or fishing tale, but a one-time employer later described him as lazy and irresponsible. "Put him alongside a pile of work and he'd never touch it unless he had somebody pushing him along. He was always buying all kinds of fishing equipment and when he came back he could tell the damnedest stories you ever heard."

Pattan fell behind on rent for their apartment in a federal housing project, for which he qualified as a veteran. Portia Lee did the arithmetic and found they owed about $3,000, nearly $28,000 in today's dollars, substantially more than the $2,400 annual salary he had earned as a game warden. She packed up, vowing not to return until he changed his ways.

Pattan told lawmen at the time of the fire that he had set it to get a job fighting it, a practice common enough to have its own name: job fire. Arsonists deliberately light fires for a bewildering variety of reasons that range from casual recklessness to murder and all points in between, but getting a job on the fire is an enduring motive. A half-century later, Pattan made a different point. He told me he was thinking about more than a job; what he intended, he said, was to clear out some of the "rank brush" that had come to blanket the mountains and canyons west of Willows. The brush or chaparral – a mixed collection of chamise, manzanita, whitethorn, redbud, Christmas berry, scrub oak, gray pine, and greasewood – had taken over vast sections of the Mendocino National Forest after the Big Burn of 1910, the great fire of northern Idaho and northwestern Montana that killed no fewer than eighty-five people, blackened more than three million acres, and spurred the Forest Service to adopt a blanket policy of immediately suppressing all fires on sight, affecting wildlands and public policy to this day.

Fire suppression was carried out with effect on the Mendocino National Forest. The Forest Service began keeping fire records for the forest the very next year in 1911, and from that date there is no mention of fire at the site of the Rattlesnake Fire until 1953, the year of the fire. At that time there was a brush buildup at least four decades old, perhaps much longer.

The brush was more than just a nuisance. Left unchecked, chaparral becomes an interlocking spider web of brambles and thorns that soaks up moisture, kills grass, and forms a nearly impenetrable barrier to man and beast. Irrigation water vanishes. Game disappears and predators such as cougars flourish, picking off deer and other game at the remaining water sources that are surrounded by abundant cover. Hikers and travelers have to skirt the stuff. When dried out, chaparral can burn with white-hot intensity.

Many local people came to hate the brush, and hate the Forest Service along with it. There was much talk about burning the brush, and more than talk: malicious burning became a perennial problem in California, (and it still is today). Incendiary fuel, high winds, hot weather, and more than a few fire-batty residents combine to make the state the nation's capital for wildland fire arson, meaning fires started with malicious intent and not simple negligence.

One of the most notorious arson fires in history burned in southern California in 2006 – the Esperanza Fire, which killed the five-man crew of Forest Service Engine 57 as they tried to defend a home on a near barren, only lightly populated ridge face in the San Gorgonio (Banning Pass) area east of Riverside. A local auto mechanic arrested less than a week later for setting the fire, Raymond Oyler, became the first person ever to be convicted of first-degree murder and sentenced to death for setting a wildland fire.[1]

---

[1] In a bizarre case that is arson-murder only in name, Cary Thomas Meeks pleaded guilty to second-degree murder for accidentally setting a 1997 fire in California near the Banning or San Gorgonio Pass. Meeks tossed a firework that ignited the Hemlock Fire, which burned 3,700 acres.

A veteran helicopter pilot, Floyd Hiser, working for a company under contract to the Forest Service, was killed while fighting the fire when his helicopter lost power and crashed in the San Bernardino Mountains. Moments before the crash, Hiser called over the radio, "Mayday ... I have flameout ... I'm going down." Meeks was convicted and received a startlingly mild sentence of three months probation, indicating a judgment of reduced responsibility for the death. But was Meeks responsible for the death at all? Four years later in 2001, an Orange County jury held that the manufacturer, Bell Helicopter Textron, Inc., had caused Hiser's death: Bell had installed a dangerously faulty fuel system in that model. They awarded Hiser's widow $8.7 million, and an appeals court affirmed the judgment two years later.

Meeks, however, was no innocent. He had several subsequent run-ins with the law, and then on August 3, 2013, he went on a rampage in and around San Bernardino. Over the course of two hours, Meeks slashed the throat of a 61-year-old man, who survived, and then carjacked a vehicle and its 73-year-old male driver. During a high-speed chase with police he let the 73-year-old man go after telling him he intended to kill himself. Meeks then proceeded to do exactly that, police said, by deliberately running his vehicle into a freeway pillar at more than 100 miles an hour.

The earliest support for Pattan's brush-burning excuse for setting the fire came immediately after the fire. In a page 1 note to readers, the *Willows Journal* described the long-standing controversy about the federal policy of full fire suppression: "Last week's tragic forest fire has brought to a head long held differences of opinion between a substantial number of residents in this area and the U.S. Forest Service. They center around the question of whether brush on the forest's fringe should be burned out annually or left to grow."

In an accompanying article in the newspaper, Charles "Chick" Gleeson, a *Journal* reporter who was present at the fire and witnessed the fatal moments, described in romantic terms the practices of the 19th century, when sheepherders and other stockmen regularly burned the hills. "The last man out each fall set fire to the forest as he went along, and he returned in the spring to a country of green canyons and glades open as far as the eye could see," Gleeson wrote.

In 1953 the Forest Service believed that most fires, based on the best science of the day, harmed the soil and the forest, which added authority to the agency's fire-suppression policy. "Heat can close the soil's pores," a Forest Service official told Gleeson. "It destroys the soil bacteria necessary for plant growth. It creates ideal erosion conditions." Whether the science was right or wrong – probably half one, half the other – the Forest Service's policy was to suppress all fires.

Pattan says he had no plan of action when he set out for the mountains that day. "It was kind of a spur-of-the-moment thing," he told me. "I didn't pre-plan. I was devastated from this problem I was having with my wife and I went to the mountains to get out of the valley, just to get away from it, just to think. And then I got up there and thought about this damn brush. I didn't dream anybody would go down in that rank brush fighting the fire."

Pattan did not intend or expect to kill anyone (unlike Oyler, the Esperanza arsonist, a serial fire-starter described by the prosecutors as "a man bent on destruction"), but Pattan's explanation sounded just a little hollow. When asked why he'd broken decades of public silence and agreed to talk to me, Pattan replied, "You said you were writing a book. I thought this might be a good way to get my side of it out."

THE MOST IMMEDIATE EFFECTS of the Rattlesnake Fire were of a human dimension: a heavy loss of life. The Rattlesnake Fire killed fifteen members of a fire crew; fourteen of them were members of the New Tribes Mission that trained for rugged service abroad at a boot camp on the Mendocino National Forest. One other was a Forest Service ranger.

That number of fifteen stood for sixty years as a marker for wildland firefighter deaths in a single event until 2013, when nineteen members of the Granite Mountain Interagency Hotshot Crew were killed on the Yarnell Hill Fire near Prescott, Arizona – a stunning reproach to safety practices in wildland firefighting. Not since the Big Burn had more wildland firefighters been killed – the eighty-five in 1910.

Although twenty-nine men were killed fighting the Griffith Park Fire of October 3, 1933 in Los Angeles, they were not a fire crew but unemployed men of the Great Depression, given a day's work rebuilding roads in the municipal park. The roadwork paid 40 cents an hour and there were plenty of takers: 3,784 men were on the rolls that day and thousands of them wound up in Griffith Park. A small blaze, almost certainly human-caused, ignited in a narrow gulch: a man in a suit was seen walking away from the fire site shortly before flames were spotted, but no one was ever caught for the crime. Some men volunteered to go into the gulch to fight it, others were ordered to go, and some reportedly were bullied and kicked into going. But the Griffith Park Fire occurred in a city park, the men were not firefighters, and their deaths were considered more a phenomenon of the hard times than a landmark for firefighters, like the Rattlesnake Fire.

The fourteen missionaries who were killed on the Rattlesnake Fire may seem similarly distant from today's world of wildland fire, but they were part of a dedicated fire crew and they accepted – even welcomed as gainful service – the occasional role as wildland firefighters. As missionaries, however, they had an outlook about life and death that set them apart, not only on account of their spiritual beliefs but also based on the New Tribe Mission's past experience: the organization already had suffered a series of violent deaths in working with primitive tribes in other countries. A decade earlier in its first full year of existence, 1943, New Tribes had sent a group of missionaries into the Bolivian jungle, where natives murdered five of them. Such a blow would have ended many an enterprise, but a year later New Tribes established its missionary boot camp at Fouts Springs on the Mendocino. Two years later, in 1946, a wooden dormitory at the camp burned to the ground and killed the infant daughter of a missionary couple.

More deaths followed. New Tribes bought a DC-3 to fly missionaries to South America; it crashed into the top of a mountain in Venezuela in bad weather on June 9, 1950. The crash killed all fifteen people aboard. Undeterred, the mission bought a replacement aircraft, and five months later, on November 21, 1950, it took off on its maiden voyage from Chico, California, carrying mission personnel to foreign posts. On board was the founder of New Tribes, Paul Fleming, along with two widows and six children of those who had crashed in Venezuela, plus nine others. The aircraft struck a ridge near the 12,694-foot peak of Mount Moran in Grand Teton National Park, within sight of the popular tourist destination of Jackson Lake. It wasn't until late the next summer that the snowy, high-altitude weather tempered enough to allow anyone to reach the crash site. Some of the bodies never were found.

Then in the summer of 1951 another New Tribes missionary was found dead, with a spear sticking out of his body, on a riverbank in the jungle near the Brazil-Bolivia border. The long, delicate spear, beautifully crafted, is included in an exhibition on a wall at the mission's headquarters hotel in Sanford, Florida.

New Tribes Mission continued to suffer losses into the new century: Martin Burnham, a pilot and New Tribes missionary, was killed in a gun battle in June 2002. The gunfire erupted when Filipino soldiers attacked a Muslim guerrilla group, Abu Sayyaf, in a rescue attempt – the guerrillas had kidnapped Burnham and his wife Gracia a year before. The incident drew international attention, not least because it came so close upon the heels of the September 11, 2001, attack by Islamic terrorists upon New York City's Twin Towers. Gracia Burnham went on to write two books about her yearlong experience as a captive; she also established a foundation to minister to Muslims in the Philippines.

At the time of the Rattlesnake Fire, though, the heavy death toll there put the future of the missionary group in doubt. "What will people think?" was the reaction of many, including Ken Johnston, a mission director who later wrote the group's history. Indeed, after the Rattlesnake Fire one missionary survivor, Paul Turner, continued on in mission work but with a troubled and heavy heart, thinking that his life's course had become a mistake.

Others found that the Rattlesnake Fire brought new light to their lives. Duane Stous, another missionary survivor on the fire, looked out the next morning from a road across from the fatal site at a hazy moonscape of charred brush, blackened stobs, and exposed mineral soil. On the far slope, too far away for him to make out details, a circle of men stood around a pile of what looked like discarded store mannequins, arms and legs jutting at odd angles. The sight of the body-recovery operation plunged Stous into despair.

Then a glow started from deep inside him. His despair turned to ecstasy. "The Lord spoke to my heart," Stous said, when I found and talked to him many years later. "He was in control. I could trust Him." Stous spent the remainder of his career as a missionary and teacher in the United States and abroad, speaking often of his experience of fire, both human and divine.

"I JUST THREW IT AND LEFT."

THE MORNING WAS SUNNY AND WARM on July 9, 1953, when the twenty-six-year-old Pattan drove west out of Willows for the foothills of the Coast Range. He had not dressed for outdoor work; he wore a yellow T-shirt, jeans, and moccasins. For an unemployed man with a family to support, he drove a very fancy car: a green 1949 Buick with whitewall tires, for which he was one payment behind.

The Buick was a memorable sight, with its elegant saloon body, sloping trunk, and distinctive grille – chrome teeth in a fat-cat smile – and it contributed to Pattan's undoing. Those who saw the Buick that day had no trouble remembering it. Inside the car were a .22 rifle, a powerboat motor, an unopened half pint of whiskey for emergencies, and several boxes of matches. (Pattan was a heavy smoker but no drinker – that would come later.)

The view from Willows in any direction is oceanic. Six million years ago the northern end of the Central Valley of California was a saltwater bay, and the flatness today is mind-numbing. Roads go on for miles without a bend. The slightest haze can obscure the Sierra Nevada mountain range to the east and the Coast Range to the west, causing you to feel as if you're actually at sea, gazing at a limitless horizon.

As Pattan headed out, he left behind the floodplain of the Sacramento River with its soppy rice checks, as the square and shallow rice-growing catchments are called. In dried fields stood endless rows of walnut, almond, plum, and peach trees, their trunks painted white to prevent sunburn, and acres upon acres of grapes, beets, onions, tomatoes, and sunflowers. A dozen miles beyond town toward the mountains to the west, the flatness gave way to soft hills speckled with oaks and marked by deep creases and folds – as though a mighty sea were heaving underneath the soil – evidence of mudslides brought on in part by erosion caused by long-term cattle grazing. The grass on the hillsides was short and dry.

The bridge over Stony Creek today, where Hwy 162 turns north toward Chrome.

A half hour's drive took Pattan to a bridge over Stony Creek, a sparkling stream in the foothills of the Coast Range that runs parallel to the mountains. He immediately turned north on the Chrome road, which follows the creek toward the tiny community of Chrome.

Another five miles brought him to another bridge, this one over Grindstone Creek, a tributary of Stony Creek. Grindstone Creek offered good fishing higher up in Grindstone Canyon, a funnel-shaped trench of colossal proportions extending more than twenty miles to Mendocino Pass, at the crest of that range. Thick chaparral kept casual anglers out of the canyon, but Pattan knew its hidden ways. He stopped on the bridge for a look; the water appeared discouragingly low for fishing.

He considered driving on a few miles to ask again for a job at Setzer's lumber mill, where he had been turned down a few days before. There was nothing for him back in Willows except a shoddy, empty apartment. He felt blocked and frustrated at every turn.

He got back in the Buick then and drove on, passing a roadside cemetery with weathered grave markers, some dating to the 1870s and bearing the names of early ranch families – Ellis, Millsap, Powell. If the sight triggered cautionary reflections on mortality for Pattan, they did not show up in his subsequent actions that day. A few miles farther on, he turned onto Hull Road, a direct track that leads past ranches and fields and up into the mountains.

The Buick rattled across a cattle guard marking the start of the climb into the forested foothills. The road forked a few hundred yards ahead at a bushy oak tree, which still stands sentinel a half-century later. Pattan pulled into one fork and turned the Buick around. It was a few minutes past noon. He picked up a box of matches and held it and the steering wheel with the same hand. With the other hand, he struck a match and flicked it out the passenger window, into the grass near the oak tree.

"I just threw it and left," he later told Clyde Larimer, the Glenn County district attorney. He pulled away fast – he always put the car in low gear and stomped on the gas pedal when starting up; it was his way of marking turf. He made it back to the main road without being seen and again crossed the bridge over Grindstone Creek. At a nearby house on the right, a man on the porch was keeping a leisurely watch on the road. Pattan pulled off and stopped. The sky was clear of smoke.

"Any fish in this creek?" Pattan called out to the man, "Tarzan" Tankersley, a logger who, despite his nickname, was of slim build. Tankersley's wife, Irene Mae, had been picking cucumbers and squash in the garden when the Buick had passed the house earlier. "I seen a boy drive it," she said later. The sight had struck her as odd, such a young man in such a fine car.

As Pattan and Tankersley chatted about fishing, a siren wound up in the distance. Pattan was the first to call attention to it, according to Tankersley's later account.

"Must be the radio," Tankersley said.

"No, it's not coming from the radio," Pattan insisted.

A California Department of Fire (CDF) pickup truck soon came into sight, siren shrieking, followed by a fire engine with men hanging on to the back. One of the men waved and pointed toward the back of the house.

The Tankersley place in 2018

"Let's look at the fire," Pattan said. He and Tankersley walked from the porch and Pattan pointed west to the foothills, where a column of smoke had materialized. Tankersley, alarmed by the sight, said he'd better get back to his job, because if the fire grew big enough, he and other loggers surely would be called to fight it, a common way in those days to assemble a fire crew of experienced woodsmen.

Pattan declared he would drive to the fire and volunteer for the crew. He had fought fires before, he said; his father, Philip, was in the Forest Service.

The first person to report the smoke was Richard Casaurang, an assistant CDF ranger based at the Fire Control Station in the tiny town of Elk Creek, about seven miles to the south. Casaurang sighted a smoky haze at 12:20 p.m. and called it in to Thelma Miller at the Elk Creek Butte Lookout, on a ridge above the town.

Casaurang then jumped in his pickup truck and switched on the siren. He arrived at what came to be called the Chrome Fire, named after the nearby town, 19 minutes later at 12:39 p.m.

The site of Elk Creek Butte Lookout today

Casaurang immediately suspected arson. Burning in low grass, the blaze covered several acres and had spread slowly up the slope from the road. How else could it have started? There had been no lightning in the region for over a month. The humidity was about 30 percent, high enough to discourage a fire. There was no sign of a campfire anywhere in the vicinity.

"Had to be a match," Casaurang said later.

He and the CDF engine crew began to dig a break around the fire's edge.

Pattan, meanwhile, thought it might be too obvious if he showed up immediately at the fire he had set. Instead, he drove from the Tankersley place in the opposite direction, toward the Elk Creek Butte Lookout; from there, he would have a good view of the fire's progress without incriminating himself. By the time Pattan reached the lookout, Thelma Miller was a busy woman.

She and her husband Archie, a firefighter for the Forest Service, had been eating lunch when she'd received Casaurang's initial smoke report. Thelma looked out the window – there were forty windows in the lookout, a standard size, each one requiring weekly washing – and saw haze to the north. Within thirty seconds it had coalesced into a smoke column. She radioed the Mendocino National Forest headquarters in Willows and reported the fire, which appeared to be on state, not federal, land.

"Roll the state," replied Harley Ripley, the Forest Service dispatcher, adding that Archie might as well go, too. Fires didn't respect bureaucratic boundaries, the flames could well spread to federal land, and helping out another agency was good policy on its own. As Thelma telephoned CDF firefighters, Archie left his meal behind and headed for his truck.

Pattan showed up at the lookout just minutes after Archie had departed, offering the convenient lie that he had seen smoke while in the town of Elk Creek and had come up for a better view. He and Miller watched as the smoke column boiled and thickened. If the fire burned into Grindstone Canyon, Pattan remarked, "it'll go like hell."

When Miller asked him who he was, he said his name was Pattan. "I guess you know my dad," he said.

Miller said yes, of course, she knew Phil Pattan. Everybody knew Phil.

As they watched, the smoke stopped churning, then thinned out and turned white.

The old line of scrub oaks at the origin of the Chrome Fire

The Chrome Fire was becoming another in a long series of failures for Pattan. Over the lookout radio they heard CDF firefighters describing flames dying down after scorching a paltry eleven acres of grass. The fire burned around but did not fatally damage a row of scrub oak trees. A firefighter's hand-drawn map from that day shows a string of Xs for the trees, which remained standing in a ghostly line a half-century later.

Pattan hung around the lookout for a half hour or more. The excitement drained away, replaced by nervous emptiness. At some point, he signed the lookout's visitor register, perhaps out of boredom, perhaps to act as though he had nothing to hide, or perhaps to establish an alibi should he need one. Miller, preoccupied with her duties, did not notice when he left.

Pattan drove in to Elk Creek, stopped at the Elkhorn Tavern, and bought himself a beer. The bartender, Edward Howard, remembered glancing at a wall clock as Pattan came in the door: it was 2 p.m. Pattan perked up a little when Howard recognized him. "This is Phil Pattan's boy," Howard said, introducing him around. Having Phil Pattan's son in the tavern was such an event that the bartender bought Pattan a second beer.

The Elkhorn Tavern in Elk Creek

Pattan left the bar shortly thereafter. The day was warm but not hot. A gentle breeze blew from the southeast. The mercury reached into the upper eighties, far short of the record-setting temperatures of the coming days, which would soar into the triple digits after a major weather shift. That shift came with sudden and terrible force just a few hours later.

Pattan drove north again, this time turning west sooner than the time before, and headed back toward the mountains on Alder Springs Road, which runs parallel to and just south of Grindstone Canyon. He drove about four miles up, to a hairpin turn called Oleta Point, halfway up a short canyon that branches off Grindstone Canyon. The short canyon, a mile and a half long, lies between two ridges, Rattlesnake Ridge to the south and Powderhouse Ridge to the north. Powderhouse was named for a Forest Service dynamite shed tucked away on its north side, overlooking Grindstone Canyon. Local names vary, but in this story the short in-between canyon will be called Powderhouse Canyon.

Oleta Point, origin of the Rattlesnake Fire

Pattan, bored, frustrated, and with two beers in him, took out the .22 rifle. Brush was the only target and he aimlessly fired several shots into it. The crack of the rifle echoed emptily across the vast canyon and died away without effect. He got back in the Buick and retraced his route back to Elk Creek, this time stopping for a quick milkshake at the Green Room Café, mixing sugar with the unaccustomed alcohol. Back in the Buick, he retraced his route to Oleta Point, and again took out the .22 and shot into the canyon, scattering more brass shell casings. His mood at the time, he said later, was not angry or mean, but everything that day had reminded him of his failures – as a son, a husband, a worker, and now even as a fire starter.

Pattan climbed back into the Buick and dug out a box of matches. He shifted into low gear and gunned the engine, managing to hold the steering wheel and light the match at the same time. He drove less than a hundred yards – 240 feet by later measurement – before flipping the match out the driver's window. He couldn't have been traveling too fast because the match didn't go out. When I first met Pattan he demonstrated in his living room for me the gesture he had made in throwing the match out the window of his car. His eyes took on a hooded look and his arm lashed out in alarming resemblance to the swift strike of a rattlesnake.

The flaring match landed in chaparral on the uphill side of the road, which meant the fire could burn upward, its natural path, without the road acting as a break. An observer would give much to know what had been going through Pattan's mind during these critical seconds; it's dangerous territory trying to enter the mind of someone who commits a desperate act like this one that goes horribly wrong.

When I first wrote about this moment I described Pattan as being full of venom and frustration, acting in the heat of the moment. After the story was published and Pattan had read it, we talked again. The story had brought back many unwanted memories and he was upset, but he said the only thing I'd gotten wrong was his state of mind when he lit the match. "It wasn't like that," he said. He hadn't been raging within, he told me. He had been in possession of himself and had acted without heat or malice.

WHEN PATTAN CONFESSED LATER in Willows, the only reason he gave for setting the fire was to make work for himself.

"And now, just tell us again, like I told you before, honestly – why did you start the fires?" District Attorney Larimer asked.

"I needed the work and the money," Pattan replied.

"Is that the reason why you started the fires?"

"That is the reason why I started the fires."

It's perhaps too much to ask someone like Pattan to search for deeper motives in himself and in his act of arson – such as a failure to live up to his father, a failure to stick with a game warden job he loved, a sense of the grandiose in his storytelling that was not sustainable in the everyday world, or the breakup of his marriage. Motives get mixed the deeper they run, and Pattan was a mass of deep-seated frustrations. He had acted on impulsive feelings that found expression in a reckless act of criminal negligence, with an undercurrent of premeditation evident in his setting the earlier Chrome Fire. He tried twice to light a fire, but there is evidence that he hadn't headed for the mountains with fully formed intent to do the deed. He started the day in town clothes, not in work clothes for fighting fires. He wandered around the mountain roads, stopping here and there, telling easily disproved lies, and leaving his name in the lookout register. He drove to Oleta Point twice before he struck the fateful match. These are not the actions of a man who sets out to do as much harm as possible, one who fits the mold of a "man bent on destruction."

Pattan was in a disturbed mental state. Even those who arrested and interrogated him, Sheriff Lyle Sale and County District Attorney Clyde Larimer, expressed understanding or sympathy for the depth of his confusion. The last words recorded in the transcript of their final interview with Pattan, after the pair had extracted a complete confession, were these:

SALE: Stanford, is there anything else that you might want to tell us that we have not asked you?

PATTAN: No, all I did (hesitation) ... I didn't (hesitation) ...

LARIMER: I think what you want to say is you certainly didn't intend to kill anybody. What you intended to do was start a fire and get a job on it. You didn't know that anybody was going to be burned to death?

PATTAN: Yes.

LARIMER: Is that it?

PATTAN: That's it. Yeah.

Is there a shred of evidence that Pattan had a moment's thought at the time, as he later claimed, about burning brush for the common good?

As a matter of fact, there is. The brush offers its own mute testimony. It was a forbidding gray barrier stretching to the horizon, depriving Pattan of his most reliable pleasures in life, hunting and fishing. He literally shot the brush with his a rifle, transferring frustration about his personal life onto it, however ineffectually. He no doubt shared the common attitude, recorded in Gleeson's story a week later, that the Forest Service was acting against local interests in allowing the brush to build up.

Also tellingly, after the shock of the fatalities and his arrest had had a chance to wear off, Pattan gave a probation officer a fuller account of why he had started the fires, and he specifically cited brush burning as a goal. He had left Willows to look for work in a lumber mill, he said, but "there was none." He didn't know what to do with himself, except he had thought of "starting a brush fire."

"I had in the past heard a lot of people say it would be a good thing if Grindstone Canyon would burn off, and I knew I could get work of some kind on it. I have never started a fire and it took a lot of willpower for me to do it. I was desperate at the time."

Pattan, then, at least mentioned brush burning as a motive for arson at the time. As to what he was thinking during the fateful moments, the answer most probably is: not much. The fire was his attempt to escape internal trauma, a sense of being overwhelmed, for which the canyon-choking "rank brush" made a worthy metaphor.

After tossing the match, Pattan drove off without a backward glance.

THE FIRE

THE FIRST PERSON TO SEE THE SMOKE from the Rattlesnake Fire was Archie Miller; after he left Elk Creek Butte Lookout, his wife, and his dinner, he drove to the Chrome Fire. The CDF crew, supplemented by a few Forest Service firefighters, had matters there well in hand, so Miller drove back the way he had come, except this time he turned west onto Alder Springs Road, just as Pattan had only minutes earlier. Miller had barely started up the road when he saw a thread of smoke rising from the mountains ahead. He estimated that the smoke was about four miles up the canyon (an accurate guess: it was measured at 4.1 miles a few days later). From that distance, he said later, the fire under the smoke appeared to be small, about "three times bigger than a man's hat."

Miller hurriedly drove on, hoping to find a telephone at the Gillaspy ranch at the mouth of Powderhouse Canyon, a short mile below the fire. The ranch phone, though, was out of order. So Miller set up his radio, a bulky affair with a whip aerial, and tried to raise Thelma at the lookout.

"Thelma, have you seen this smoke way down from Powderhouse Turn?" he asked, as he later related to investigators.

He heard no answer but described the fire anyway, in case Thelma could hear him. Thelma, it turned out, did hear him, but she was busy taking a reading on the smoke she had just spotted.

"Wait a minute," she answered, but the message didn't get through to Archie.

"I hollered at her a time or two," he later said. "No answer. So the time was precious. I just about halfway throwed my radio back together and beat it up the hill." By the time he reached the fire, it had grown considerably larger than three hats.

"I saw it was too big for one man to handle," Miller said. Flames had spread twenty-five to thirty feet up the steep slope. Miller drove past the flames, hunting for an unobstructed place to set up the radio again. When he finally made contact with Thelma, he learned that she already had passed the fire report on to the Forest Service headquarters in Willows. Her call was logged there at 2:40 p.m. Two minutes later, firefighters on the Chrome Fire reported that their blaze was under control (it wasn't; the fire flared up that night and only then was brought under control). Men working at the Chrome Fire and others en route, though, were diverted to the Rattlesnake Fire, which meant they had the lucky break of catching that fire early – delay in getting there was never an issue.

"Yes, men are rolling," Thelma told her husband. "Men are coming to the fire."

Archie headed back to Oleta Point and the base of the fire. By then, flames had blackened an area in the shape of a massive first baseman's mitt, a V with a narrow, blackened bottom at Alder Springs Road and a wide, irregular top. Two other firefighters had arrived and had started up to attack the fire: Julio Silva, a Forest Service ranger, and his helper David Pesonen, at age nineteen probably the youngest man to fight the fire.

Alder Springs Road wraps around Oleta Point. The fire's origin, where Pattan threw out the match, is the small crescent of grass on the uphill side of the road, on the right side of the photo. The fire burned uphill and involved the draw on the left.

Pesonen revisited the site decades later and walked the ground with me. "I'd been on the job a week," he told me. "No training, just a healthy body, and I knew how to use a shovel. Here was a *huge* fire just taking off up the mountainside. We couldn't *possibly* do anything with it. We called for help."

In 1953 Pesonen was a young man on the loose. He had graduated with a forestry degree from the University of California at Berkeley and then bummed around for a while. He had taken his first real job a few days before, as a tank truck operator for the Forest Service, under the tutelage of Silva at the Alder Springs station several miles west of the fire site. He had driven to Willows earlier in the day for a job-related physical examination, and he was driving back to Alder Springs – he'd passed Oleta Point minutes before Pattan set the fire there – when he saw Silva in a truck "coming around a corner hell-bent for leather."

"We've got a fire," said Silva, who told Pesonen to throw his gear in the truck, a Dodge Power Wagon with a slip-on pumper unit. It would be Pesonen's first and most memorable fire experience, though he would later go on to train as a smokejumper. After an injury on a practice jump ended that experience, he became a lawyer and anti-nuclear activist and was eventually appointed the director of the CDF under Governor Jerry Brown – he went from grunt-level firefighter to the man in charge of California's formidable firefighting corps. As CDF director, he returned to the Mendocino National Forest and had a reunion with Silva, which included a predictable joke about how Silva had taught Pesonen everything he knew.

PESONEN AND SILVA HAD BEEN DRIVING together toward the fire for only a minute or two when they came around a curve and there, not thirty yards ahead, was a green Buick making a fast turn onto a little-used side road. Pesonen glimpsed the Buick's rear license plate.

"Remember these things," Silva instructed him. Two fires in the same general area on a calm day with no lightning could well mean arson, Silva said. And it was odd to see a luxury sedan heading off on that rugged side road, which led to Long Point Lookout and then down to the bottom of Grindstone Canyon. Pesonen scratched the license plate number on a slip of paper and stuffed it in his pocket.

The pair drove on and arrived at Oleta Point about 3:15 p.m. By then the flames had extended beyond the reach of the hose on their truck. Silva radioed for a bulldozer and more men, then he and Pesonen grabbed a brush hook and a root ripper and started up the steep slope at the side of the road. Silva called a halt within minutes. The slope was nearly sheer, the dense brush was close to impenetrable, and the fire had too much of a head start. They slid and stumbled back to Alder Springs Road.

By then, a large contingent of men and vehicles had gathered along the road, including Charles 'Charlie' Lafferty. A veteran Forest Service fire control officer, he'd heard the fire report over the radio in his pickup truck, and as he drove to the location another call came in that assigned him to the fire. He was senior and took charge. "I talked to the boys and told them to follow me," Lafferty said later. He led them to the head of Powderhouse Canyon, to a second hairpin turn, Powderhouse Turn. It was locally infamous for flipping logging trucks, and created a wide pullout with a sweeping view. The pullout instantly became the fire command post.

Jack Ewing, a senior Forest Service supervisor, joined them there within minutes. At Mendocino headquarters he'd been assigned as fire boss, and he took over from Lafferty, who became number two, or line boss in charge of operations. Ewing was "one of the most experienced brush fire men in the California region," according to the official fire report. The reputation had come at a price, however, for Ewing was a man with a past.

A decade earlier, on October 2, 1943, Ewing had been fire boss when eleven U.S. Marines were killed and seventy-two others injured while fighting the Hauser Creek Fire on the Cleveland National Forest in southern California. In the aftermath, Ewing was held partly responsible for the deaths. The fire had started from marine gunnery practice, and the marines turned out in numbers to fight it. Ewing put more than a hundred marines in the charge of Buel Hunt, a relatively inexperienced subordinate, and sent them off to attack the fire on one of its flanks. Ewing went to attend to other duties and never checked back on Hunt and his marine crew.

The wind shifted unexpectedly – exactly what would happen a decade later in Powderhouse Canyon – and flames overran the marines. They tried to shelter on a boulder-strewn hillside, but the fire burned over its eighty-three victims, killing eleven of them. The official report cited Ewing for making a serious error of judgment when he "over-appraised" Hunt's abilities. Hunt bore the heaviest responsibility, according to the report, because he had acted "imprudently" in constructing a fireline too close to the main fire. But Ewing should have kept a closer check on Hunt and his men, and that error too would be echoed in Powderhouse Canyon. The Hauser Creek report cites both Ewing and Hunt for negligence in language remarkably accusatory for the day, a time when fire deaths were considered acts of nature and fire bosses virtually beyond reproach.

"It is at least a question whether one of them might not have been spared for a time long enough to check the location of the line selected for initial attack, to check fire behavior for a longer period than that done by Ewing before Hunt's assignment to the east line, and to appraise the early results of the attack on that flank," said the report, edging close to sarcasm.

The report recommended no disciplinary action, however, against either man. It excused them with an argument unthinkable in today's world: "Few of the seasoned senior officials of unquestioned firefighting ability have reached their present status without narrow escapes of themselves and their men, comparable in everything but tragic consequences, with Hunt's situation on this fire. *The training of fully dependable high caliber leadership demands this rather rugged and at times brutal process.*" [emphasis added]

By 1953 memories of Hauser Creek had blurred, or at least there is no mention of it in the Rattlesnake report, no looking back and linking the two events.

When Ewing took charge of the fire, he had about fifteen men at his command and many more on the way. Miller, Silva, and Pesonen were the first to reach the site; Casaurang and a crew from the Chrome Fire showed up shortly afterward, as did Robert Powers, assistant ranger from the Alder Springs station, plus two others from there: Robert Werner (who would later bring a lifetime of comfort to a bereaved family), and Harry Simpson.

It was about 4 p.m. when this group gathered at Powderhouse Turn, with its panoramic view, to plan an attack. The fire had been burning for an hour and a half and was putting up a narrow but dense smoke plume. Its base was nearly a mile down the canyon from the Turn.

Aerial view of the fire site looking downcanyon to the east.

The firefighters decided to start from the Turn and box in the fire on three uphill sides. The fire was burning as expected up the canyon, so the men had little concern for its downcanyon side. It was a classic and well-tested plan: establish an anchor point, flank the fire, and pinch it off at its head.

Alder Springs Road provided one firebreak; it became the lower flank. All the flames were above the road, not down in the canyon. Ewing stationed men and vehicles along the road to prevent embers from spilling over it and toward the bottom of the canyon, which could turn the place into a furnace. Fire below the road could sweep all of Powderhouse Canyon, engulf Powderhouse Turn, and even spill over north into Grindstone Canyon, with no natural features to stop a fire for miles.

Simultaneously, a crew with hand tools was sent to construct a firebreak along the ridge top on the south flank above the fire. That would keep flames from slopping over into the next drainage on the south, Rattlesnake Creek, the landmark that gave the fire its name. (The ridge where the fire occurred is referred to in Forest Service documents and court testimony as Rattlesnake Ridge, and will be so identified here, though detailed Forest Service maps identify Rattlesnake Ridge more specifically as the next one over to the south, and there's also disagreement about that.)

Those two firelines, along Alder Springs Road and on Rattlesnake Ridge, would contain the fire's flanks. Meanwhile, a third line would be cut in front of the fire's path, taking off straight up from Powderhouse Turn to a place aptly named High Point, a peak on Rattlesnake Ridge. Together, the three lines would box in and contain the fire, in theory forcing it to burn itself out.

Once the lines were well established, crews using fusees would light fires along Alder Springs Road and the fireline constructed up from Powderhouse Turn to cut off the fire's advance. There was no need to set fire along the top of Rattlesnake Ridge because fires do not readily burn downhill, except in the most unusual of circumstances – but then, a wildfire by definition is "wild" and no more predictable than the wind.

It was a good plan. A half-century later in 2001 thirty seasoned CDF firefighters toured the site with me, taking on the roles of the Rattlesnake firefighters – the first large-scale "staff ride" conducted at the site, to our collective knowledge, but certainly not the last. We came up with no better plan of attack. The 1953 plan worked, too, until darkness fell, the wind grew antic, and the men forgot the tricks that a fire can play – and even forgot one another for a few crucial minutes. But as long as daylight lasted, the plan for the Rattlesnake Fire proved a grand success.

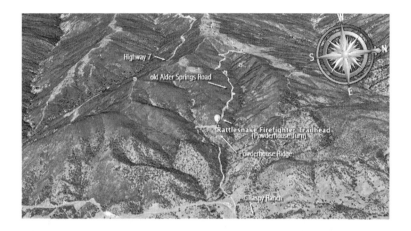

Looking west up toward Mendocino Pass from the bottom of the canyon.
Powderhouse Ridge is the short spur ridge where the "firefighter trailhead" is sited.

"THERE'S A HELL OF A FIRE."

THOUGH PATTAN HAD TOSSED HIS MATCH and driven off without a look back, he yearned to see the effect of his handiwork, a compulsion that has tripped up many an arsonist. The Chrome Fire had quickly died out, but perhaps this second one would be his longed-for success. Pattan drove west, into the mountains, for nearly six miles and then turned onto the side road toward Long Point Lookout, where he was spotted by Silva and Pesonen and his Buick's license number noted. Long Point Lookout is perched on the end of a ridge that sticks out like a thumb into Grindstone Canyon. Fifty years later, the only sign of the fourteen-foot-high lookout cabin, which had been sited flat on the ground and had no stairs, is a crumbling concrete foundation with tufts of chaparral sprouting inside. The place has an eagle's view. On a clear day you can see miles down Grindstone Canyon to the east, and miles to the crest of the Coast Range to the west. Even on a calm day, the wind here can take off your hat.

Pattan saw a curl of smoke from the Rattlesnake Fire rising over the lip of Grindstone Canyon, the spot that marked the top of Powderhouse Canyon. Firefighters would be there by now, he figured; he had noted how quickly they'd responded to the Chrome Fire. But the fire would not be big enough yet to justify hiring temporary firefighters such as Pattan. The flames needed time to spread.

He drove past the lookout to the bottom of Grindstone Canyon and stopped at a picnic table alongside the road, where he again took out his .22 and plinked at cans for a few minutes. Bored and restless, he started the Buick and drove back the way he had come, up to Alder Springs Road, heading for the Forest Service station at Alder Springs.

Pattan's Buick was becoming a familiar sight in the mountains; Silva and Pesonen were not the only ones who marked its passage to and fro. Lester Gillaspy, whose ranch lay at the mouth of Powderhouse Canyon, noticed the Buick earlier in the day, when Pattan drove up the canyon for the first time. "I saw a green Buick sedan with one man in it," Gillaspy said later. "The car was gone a short time and then came back down. I went to Elk Creek and saw the green Buick sedan was parked in front of the Green Room Café and the man inside was sitting at the counter."

Another witness that afternoon was William Brown, a Forest Service firefighter released from the Chrome Fire. On his way to the Rattlesnake Fire, Brown spotted the Buick at the bottom of Grindstone Canyon, where Pattan had parked briefly and shot at cans. When Brown saw it, it was headed up toward Alder Springs Road "going so fast all I seen was a broadside of the car. He went so fast I never could catch him." Brown noted the distinctive slope of the vehicle's trunk, but said he could not be certain of recognizing that individual car again.

As Pattan drove in to the Forest Service station at Alder Springs, after his side trip to the bottom of Grindstone Canyon, he saw two women standing outside. They were Viola Silva, Julio's wife, and Maude

Powers, whom everyone called Maudi. She was Ranger Powers' wife.

"He seemed very friendly," Mrs. Silva said later. "He asked Maudi and me how the fire was." The women told Pattan that their husbands had left moments before to fight the fire.

Mrs. Silva asked him who he was. Stan Pattan, he replied. Did she know his father, Phil?

Oh, sure, she said, everyone knew Phil Pattan.

Pattan told the women he did not want to fight the fire in the clothes he was wearing, the lightweight T-shirt, jeans, and moccasins, so he was going to bypass the fire and go home to Willows by another route.

Lawmen later pressed Pattan about the encounter with the women, trying to stir his conscience.

"Did you know the names of either of the women you talked to?" asked District Attorney Larimer.

"Well, I know Mrs. Silva. And I didn't know Mrs. Powers."

Did he ever realize he had been talking to a woman who was about to become a widow?

"Yes," Pattan replied, he had found out later about Mrs. Powers.

PATTAN DROVE A ONE-LANE BACK ROAD to Elk Creek and had to squeeze the Buick past a logging truck coming the other way.

"There's a hell of a fire down at Powderhouse Canyon," he told the loggers. "I don't want to fight fire, so I'm going down the access road."

The loggers made a joke of it, saying maybe they should turn their rig around and flee, the fire being so big. The exchange took place at 4:05 p.m., the loggers later recalled.

By then, men were converging on the Rattlesnake Fire from far and wide. The flame of a single match had raised a column of smoke that had become a guidon for battle. Men with willing arms and backs headed for the smoke from logging camps, forest stations, the Forest Service headquarters at Willows, and from a place high in the mountains removed from ordinary life.

Kids at the missionary camp in 1953 with the old fire bell.

At the missionary boot camp, tucked far away from the temptations of the world, men and women left their chores and hastily assembled at the chapel, summoned by a large bell that served as the camp's public address system. There, the motto "To Die Is to Gain" hung on a placard as a reminder of their belief that while life on earth is short, glory lies beyond the grave.

The men wore their work clothes: denim pants, long-sleeved shirts, wide belts or suspenders, and soft hats. Wives in gingham dresses came from gardens or slab-sided cabins, children on their hips or holding their hands. Girls whose faces bore no sign of makeup came to wave goodbyes to husbands, friends, sweethearts, and fiancés.

The scene had the festive air of a barn raising. It was the first fire of the season and had been eagerly anticipated; fire gear had been packed and ready for weeks. The missionaries flipped coins to decide who was lucky enough to go on the first truckload. They were glad to join together for a work of service. They had no way to see what lay ahead: natural forces with the power to turn Pattan's casual description of a "hell of a fire" into an all-too-real hell on earth: a place of anguish, torment, and devouring flames.

"He never knew a stranger."

HARLEY RIPLEY, DISPATCHER AT WILLOWS, wasted no time in ordering up the mission crew. Ripley made the call to the Fouts Springs camp within the same minute, 2:40 p.m., that the fire was reported to him. It was the second fire of the day, and Ripley needed every able body he could muster. Answering the call at the Fouts Springs mission camp was Homer Hancock, a mission director who kept a small general store there and worked for the Forest Service as a seasonal firefighter. The first truckload of twelve missionaries, plus Hancock as driver, left for the fire eleven minutes later, at 2:51 p.m., a quick start for a pickup crew even today.

The missionary trainees hailed mostly from small towns with names like Ypsilanti, North Platte, Birchdale, Ogallah, and Glendale, from across the United States and Canada. Many of the men had served in World War II and had started families immediately upon their return home; they had young children galore. Most in their twenties and thirties, the missionaries were of various Protestant denominations, but they shared a literal interpretation of the Bible and a commitment to preach the Gospel to primitive tribes who had never before seen a missionary – the "new tribes" of the mission's name. The missionaries were seekers embarked on a quest, not adolescents out for a frolic.

The missionaries were plain in appearance but they were set apart in manner. A reporter for the Chico

Enterprise-Record, Lee Soto, spent a few days at Fouts Springs just before the fire and struggled to describe exactly how they were different. "It is difficult for one from the 'natural world' to live among people who eat the same food you do, wear clothes like you, speak the same language, and can laugh – but still consider themselves to be from another world."

A child of two missionaries, George R. Baird, described in adulthood what it was like to live in a New Tribes mission camp in the mid-1950s. "What this reality meant was isolation from non-believers, constant religious meetings, no access to TV or radio, no external worldly news ... and poverty. I knew or understood little of this but accepted the reality of my life stoically," he wrote to me. Though Baird had no love for the "captive life" he was forced to live in a New Tribes training facility in Pennsylvania, he'd discovered an old file of newspaper clippings about the Rattlesnake Fire in the camp library. The story, which included graphic photographs of the dead, captured his imagination. Many decades later, in May 2012, after a career in the military and trucking business, he made a pilgrimage to the site. "My wife Linda and I lingered for several hours in the late afternoon of a beautiful day with clear skies, and I played the pipes honoring the fallen for lost lives and lost time. The pipes echoed mournfully through the valley of fire and death."

When the missionaries first arrived at Fouts Springs, a picturesque but lonely valley far back in the mountains, they were full of hope. Paul Fleming, a man with a charismatic personality or "burning heart," as Kenneth Johnston the mission historian described him, founded the New Tribes Mission in 1942. A native of Los Angeles, Fleming contracted malaria while serving as a missionary in the 1930s in what was then the British colony of Malaya – present-day Malaysia. During his recuperation he had what he called a "vision," a moment of inspiration compelling him to preach the Gospel to primitive peoples. Fleming's vision was apocalyptic, an attempt to fulfill a passage in the Gospel of Matthew 24:14, which calls upon Christians to witness "to all nations, and then the end shall come." He and his followers made a covenant committing themselves to reach "the last tribe with the Gospel in our generation," which for them meant bringing on the end of the world.

Fouts Springs today

New Tribes Mission started with few members and little money, but by November 1942 it had sent abroad its first missionary group, ten adults and six children.

This was the group that went to Bolivia, where five of them were killed the following year by the primitive tribesmen they were trying to convert. First based in Chicago, the mission turned a vacant Rush Street nightclub called the Hi Hat Club into its headquarters; over the years New Tribes would convert to their use many resorts of dubious reputation from coast to coast.

The next year in 1943, the mission launched a publication called *Brown Gold*. The title sounds patronizing and racist to the contemporary ear, but it was bravely liberal for its day, calling on Christians to treasure souls in brown bodies. As the organization grew, its members felt the need for more spacious administrative quarters and a place to train for the rigors of jungle life. Johnston, who was then a preacher in California, had known of Fouts Springs and suggested it.

The place had hosted the high life as a mineral springs resort (and by reputation a speakeasy), but that enterprise had failed with the repeal of Prohibition. During the Great Depression, the site became a base camp for the Civilian Conservation Corps, the enlightened brainchild of Franklin Roosevelt that put the army of the unemployed to work on projects in the nation's forests and parks. The CCC camp closed when World War II turned the army of unemployed into factory workers and a real army – men whose CCC training gave the U.S. Army, with its ranks diminished by inter-war cutbacks and a prevailing isolationist spirit, a much-needed jumpstart. By 1944 the Fouts Springs facilities were vacant and falling apart; that year the Forest Service offered New Tribes Mission free use of the place – 649 acres of wild country with six dilapidated

CCC buildings – in return for custodial/caretaking services on the property. Johnston gave up his pulpit and led an advance party, including his wife Lilly and their two children, to scout the place.

The cabins were not only tumbledown but lacked even basic necessities such as stoves. There were no powerlines for miles, let alone electrical hookups; another child of the Great Depression, the 1935 Rural Electrification Administration, a Roosevelt plan to bring electricity to the countryside, had not reached into the Mendocino wilderness. Water came from nearby Trout Creek; the first person to fetch it returned with a big rattlesnake that he had killed on the bank. "What tremendous possibilities!" Johnston exulted in his history, written long after this daunting introduction; there is no record of his wife's initial reaction. He was away from the camp doing public speaking at the time of the fire. The mission crew, he said, had fought fire for several years "as a public service, not to raise funds for their mission work." The mission continued to send out a fire crew for several years after the Rattlesnake Fire, he said, until it outgrew the Fouts Springs facility and moved elsewhere.[2]

The first missionary class of about one hundred came to Fouts Springs a few months later, in January 1945; the next year the entire New Tribes Mission moved there. A trip to the nearest town for groceries took a day. The fledgling missionaries learned to fish and hunt wild game, kept cows and pigs, and tended kitchen gardens. After the 1946 fire destroyed the dormitory, the

---

[2] Johnston was retired by the time I spoke to him on September 10, 2001; he died on September 23 of that year.

missionaries built their own slab-sided cabins, storage buildings, and work sheds. By 1953 there were more than sixty structures at the camp, all painted the same dull brownish red.

> New Tribes Mission, today known as Ethnos360, is an international, theologically evangelical Christian mission organization based in Sanford, Florida. NTM now has about 3,300 missionaries in more than 20 nations.
>
> ethnos360.org/about

From the start, serving on the fire crews offered those at the missionary camp a chance to contribute toward a community service in lieu of rent, a welcome diversion from their near-monastic existence, and an equally welcome chance to earn some hard cash. The men quickly established a name for themselves as firefighters; in fact they were known by several names: the missions, the mission boys, or more commonly, the mission crew. At the time of the Rattlesnake Fire, New Tribes Mission had a contract with the Forest Service to provide, day or night, "all or a portion of its employees as may be determined by the fire emergency."

The mission crew supplemented the area's better-trained state and federal crews; they were supposed to be the last called out and the first relieved. But in practice, the missionaries proved to be so eager and reliable that they were often summoned at the first sign of trouble, as happened on the Rattlesnake Fire. Leon Thomas, supervisor of the Mendocino National Forest, often sang their praises. "They are the tops," he'd say at public gatherings.

The 1953 contract, signed for the federal government by Lafferty, line boss on the fire, fixed the missionary pay at the prevailing rates of $1.30 an hour with board for an unskilled firefighter, and up to $2.48 an hour without board for the most highly skilled workers, those who packed airplane cargo. Most of the missionaries were paid at the lowest level, but the money made a big difference: at the time New Tribes could keep a missionary in the field for $60 to $90 a month – just a few days' wages with overtime for a man on the fire crew.

"We were kind of a hotshot unit," said Duane Stous, the survivor who recommitted himself to missionary work after the Rattlesnake Fire. "All the men went. It was a good deal. They paid us good, fed us good. It was exciting."

The term *hotshots* was in casual use in those days, but now is formally applied to highly trained twenty-person interagency crews who stay together all season and are considered national resources – they fight big fires anywhere in the country, from Florida to Alaska and beyond. The missionary firefighters were nothing like contemporary hotshots. They were "above average" in training for the day, the official fire report says, because "half of them had fire training or experience or both." Of course that means half of them had no training and no fire experience.

"Back in those days everything was pretty loose," Stous remembers. The Forest Service ran a rudimentary fireguard school in the spring, which some of the missionaries attended. Stous had joined the mission three days before the Rattlesnake Fire and had never fought a fire in his life. One mission firefighter had been at Fouts Springs for only a matter of hours: Paul Gifford, a supporter of New Tribes who was visiting from Vancouver, British Columbia, joined the fire crew on the spur of the moment – and paid the highest price for his decision.

The missionaries did have a few trained hands. Stanley Vote had risen to the rank of foreman as a regular "seasonal" firefighter. He had attended fireguard school and had fought wildland fire for two seasons. In recognition of this, the twenty-four-year-old wore a nickel-plated badge; regular Forest Service firefighters wore solid bronze badges, and the difference would be significant in identifying bodies in the aftermath of the Rattlesnake Fire.

Stanley Vote, whose parents were evangelical pastors in Minnesota, was a popular figure at Fouts Springs; he was engaged to another trainee, Ramona Briggs. The couple planned to travel to Thailand together as missionaries once they'd completed training and had married. Vote had a cheerful spirit and a talent for singing and playing the accordion. "He never knew a stranger," said his brother-in-law Gerald Hosterman. A letter Vote wrote from the mission camp, Hosterman said, gave a picture of "what made Stan tick." In the letter, Vote noted that the climate "is excellent for Arthritis," quoted several passages from scripture, and then stated somewhat prophetically, "My goal is God Himself, not joy, not peace, nor even blessing ... at any cost, dear Lord, by any road!"

Also among those clambering aboard the fire trucks and taking the road to the Rattlesnake Fire was Benjamin Dinnel, twenty-six, a native of Chico, a town 30 miles northeast of Willows. Dinnel had arrived at Fouts Springs just four days earlier, on a Sunday. A navy veteran with service in the South Pacific, Dinnel had spent months considering his decision to join the mission. He hoped to be sent to Africa. Dinnel's father Glenn described him as a faithful member of the Grace Baptist Church who frequently attended Youth for Christ meetings. "We wanted him to do just whatever he wanted to do," Glenn Dinnel said of his son's decision.

Others had more involved personal histories, and the fire would act as leveler, bringing them together. The missionary study course at the time lasted a year and included language, geography, and religious studies as well as rigorous hiking and camping expeditions. The basic training course has since been expanded to four years with added training in linguistics, culture, electronic communications, and aviation – missionaries often must pilot their own planes to and from their remote stations. The fire, though, would give few or no points for fitness, even to the hardiest and best trained.

Cecil (Glenn C.) Hitchcock, a twenty-year-old farm boy from eastern Colorado, had ridden horses, fed stock, and pitched hay from the time he was nine years old. "He was an excellent climber and hiker in the mountains and had an uncanny sense of direction," said his sister Mavis. Cecil was active in the First Christian Church of Englewood, teaching youth classes and singing in a quartet with Mavis, with whom he sometimes also sang duets. "He was outgoing and friendly and well liked,"

Mavis said. "He was my best buddy all through our lives together." In his last hour, racing a fire in a dark and smoky canyon, Hitchcock's strength and sense of direction carried him farther than any of the others – to within just yards of safety.

Don Schlatter and his wife Janet had gone through boot camp together at Fouts Springs two years earlier. "I had been a schoolteacher in Indiana before going to Fouts Springs Boot Camp in July of 1951 with my wife Janet and six-month-old daughter Rachel," Schlatter recounted years later. "While I was there I taught in the little government school on the premises to some of the children whose parents were in the training." After Schlatter and his wife completed the course, they returned to Indiana, where he taught school for another year before they headed back to Fouts Springs to await travel visas for Thailand. While at camp, Schlatter often joined the mission crew on fires.

"I had the experience fighting various fires during the time I was at Fouts Springs, but the specific training we had was very elementary. We were just told to follow the orders of our supervisors."

Discipline in following orders, survival training, physical fitness: none of these undoubted advantages overcame time, chance, the recklessness of one man, or the wild nature of fire. But was what happened merely a bunch of random happenings without a common explanation or the consolation of lessons learned? Unanswered questions haunt every step of this narrative, from Pattan's troubled acts of arson to the turning points in the race with fire and to the eventual tragic climax. A mass fatality on a wildland fire almost invariably requires a series of wrong turns or mistakes or simple bad luck, an accumulation of screwups, one attaching to the next in an inexorable and compounding march of fate. Why did so many things go wrong at crucial moments on this fire? Putting aside questions of blame, could the outcome have been avoided by taking note of some straightforward lessons, one or two that could guide future firefighters, save lives, and help redeem the heavy loss of life?

Pattan's unanswered question is the sad "Why?" of human failure: why did he choose that place, that time, and that way to vent his frustrations? And why were the consequences, which should have been limited to just burned brush and a job on a fire crew, so catastrophic? By improbable coincidence, arsonists with far more malicious intentions than Pattan's were touching off fires all across California on that very same day. None of the other intentional fires had fatal results.

For July 9, 1953, newspapers reported that six grass fires believed to have been set by firebugs burned 1,200 acres and threatened homes near Oroville, about forty-two miles east of Willows. More spectacularly, a "ring of firebugs" simultaneously touched off a dozen building fires in downtown Fresno, causing officials to declare a state of emergency. The National Guard was called out to protect public buildings and restore calm. The fires caused $1 million in damage; twenty-five firemen and two volunteers were overcome by smoke. But no lives were lost.

Pattan, by contrast, started his fire in nuisance brush a mile from the closest human habitation, a remote ranch. He expected that no one would be harmed.

For the missionaries, the question "Why?" goes beyond bad luck and a string of minor mistakes and missed turning points all adding up to one big mistake. It even enters the theological dimension: how could people who believed they were acting in harmony with a divine and benevolent will come to such awful ends? Schlatter and Dinnel, men of similar commitment under identical circumstances, met fates as different as they could be: one lived, one died. Was it mere chance, a roll of the dice, their own judgment calls? Or did it go beyond that, as many of the missionaries later came to believe, involving an act of divine will beyond human understanding but ultimately working for the good? "They were fine fellows," said Joe Knutson, a mission official at the time, "and we know they were willing to die if God willed it."

Those who feel no need to include a divine actor in their explanation of the universe can put aside that question and Knutson's answer. But the missionaries had dedicated themselves to the quest to reach the end of time for human life by bringing godly fire to the souls of primitive tribespeople. For the thirty mission volunteers who loaded into the trucks at Fouts Springs that day, the fire promised an interlude, a short break from the rigors of their training, a bit of excitement, and some welcome cash. Instead, the fire would bring fulfillment to their quest, though not the one of their hearts' desiring. In a few hours they would confront savage forces with not a care for them nor their message, and for nearly half of them it would mean the end of their time on earth.

"GO DOWNHILL, GO DOWNHILL!"

THE ROAD FROM FOUTS SPRINGS east toward Stonyford winds through numerous switchbacks and over steep mountains, seemingly ready in spots to slide into oblivion. It took Hancock over an hour to drive to the fire, but because the summons had been immediate, he and the first load of twelve men arrived at Powderhouse Turn at 3:55 p.m. just as Ewing, Lafferty, and the others gathered to set strategy.

Many hours of daylight lay ahead, more than enough time to catch the fire. True, the smoke had turned heavy and the fire was spreading, but it was confined to the slope of Rattlesnake Ridge above Alder Springs Road.

The flames would pause when they reached the crest of the ridge, no longer driven by the slope. If the firefighters hurried, they could establish a fireline on the crest to keep flames from lapping onto the other side.

The firefighters separated into groups to put in the three sides of the box: the line along the ridge crest, the line in front of the fire, and Alder Springs Road. There was a mix of state, federal, and private firefighters, but in general, assignments broke down like this:

Vote, with most of the mission crew and several loggers, hiked up to the crest of Rattlesnake Ridge, where they nearly lost the fire in the first minutes. As the head of the fire reached the ridge top, a tongue of flame licked over the crest and ignited brush on the far slope. Vote's men quickly slid down below the extending flames. They braced themselves against the steepness of the slope and hacked out a quick firebreak to halt the fire's spread. Not only did they contain the slopover, but the line they subsequently constructed along the ridge crest held for as long as the fire burned.

Grindstone Canyon, looking up toward Mendocino Pass

Another mixed crew built line from Powderhouse Turn up to High Point on the Rattlesnake Ridge. Red Werner, who would play a healing role after the fire, was in charge here, along with Ranger Powers.

Richard Casaurang of the CDF, who earlier had fought the Chrome Fire, volunteered to take charge along Alder Springs Road, supervising his state crew and whoever else had a vehicle, which included Silva, Pesonen, and their Dodge Power Wagon. Casaurang posted trucks, engines, and crews in a staggered line along the road, ready with hoses and pumper units if and when flames threatened the road from above or tossed embers into the canyon below.

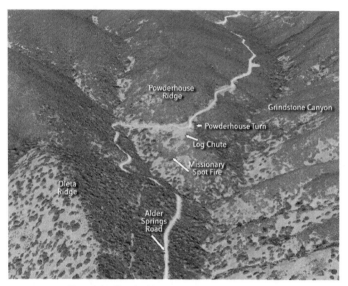

Site of the fire, looking upcanyon toward the west

Lafferty, the line boss, was everywhere. "I was up on the ridge above, and back and forth on the line-duty job," he said later. "Fire control was progressing nicely." Lafferty optimistically reported to the dispatch office in Willows that he expected early control of the fire, unless an "adverse change in weather" came along, a caution that would prove prophetic. He felt confident enough of success to leave the flames and go in search of a fire camp location; Powderhouse Turn was becoming overcrowded with bulldozers, tractors, a food truck (or candy wagon), and crews to run the equipment.

At the wheel of one truck coming around the turn at that time was none other than Stanford Philip Pattan, who had found gainful employment at last. After driving away from the mountains in midafternoon, Pattan had wandered around Willows for hours, hoping for the Rattlesnake Fire to become big enough to require extra

79

manpower. He stopped by Al Johnson's service station, where he had once worked, and asked Johnson's partner Jack Ferguson if he knew there was a fire up in the hills. Ferguson said no, he had heard nothing. Perhaps to give himself cover, Pattan suggested they drive together to inquire at Forest Service headquarters.

There, they were told the Rattlesnake Fire was nearly under control and no more men were needed, yet another keen disappointment for Pattan. He dropped Ferguson back at the service station and went on to visit his estranged wife, Portia Lee, at her parents' home. He didn't like being there, he said later, because it made him feel beholden to his in-laws. But he had cake, ice cream, and a cup of coffee. In a show of bravado, he told Portia Lee at some point – the timing varies in his accounts – that he expected to be gone for ten days or so fighting fire. After eating with his in-laws, he drove back to Johnson's service station and killed time washing the big Buick.

In early evening, unwilling to admit utter failure, Pattan returned to the Forest Service office. He hung around for an hour or so and was about to give up when, shortly after 8 p.m., reports came in of flare-ups on the Rattlesnake Fire; it was going to be an all-night campaign, at least, and the crews would need a hot breakfast. Pattan could have a job, he was told, if he didn't mind setting up a kitchen.

Pattan jumped behind the wheel of a Forest Service truck loaded with camp gear and retraced his route once again into the mountains. He reached the fire at about 9 p.m. and drove on to Camp Ellendale, a picnic ground in a grove of ponderosa pines four and a half miles west of the fire and a bit northeast of Alder Springs. Lafferty had chosen the site as a fire camp; it is a picnic ground to this day.

As Pattan made Powderhouse Turn, standing there were Thomas, the forest supervisor, and Gleeson of the *Willows Journal*. They had driven up from town together. Thomas had telephoned Gleeson in the early evening and invited the reporter to accompany him to the fire. "We've got a fire, first one of the season," Thomas said. "Thought you might like to see it." Gleeson's account of subsequent events, contained in several articles in the *Willows Journal* and in interviews with other newspapers – he was an articulate and sought-after eyewitness – has the freshest recorded memories of what was said and done during the fire.

On the drive out from Willows, Thomas told Gleeson that circumstances indicated that the fire was an arson job: two fires on the same day after weeks of no fires, and with no recent lightning or nearby campfires. The circumstances raised everyone's suspicions. Thomas had followed the progress of the Chrome Fire earlier in the day, and he expressed hope the Rattlesnake Fire would be as easy to control.

"We think we've got it hemmed in on three sides," he told Gleeson.

As they drove up Alder Springs Road, Gleeson noted that the flames were close enough for someone to "rush out and grab a burning bush." But the overall situation appeared favorable. There was an abundance of men and machines, and the backfires that had been set were now burning into the main fire. "Given any kind of a break, it seemed, the blaze would be under control within an hour or two," Gleeson estimated.

As the only passage across the mountains for many miles both north and south, Alder Springs Road remained open to traffic. Every now and then a log truck would worry its way through the fire vehicles and around Powderhouse Turn, which was no minor feat in itself. Log trucks tipped over at the hairpin turn with such regularity that the dumped logs had scraped a wide chute down the side of Powderhouse Canyon, a feature that would play a role in the coming battle.

As Gleeson and Thomas pulled up at the turn, they heard Lafferty sign off "ten four" on his radio. Lafferty had just received the latest weather report, and it was an encouraging one. The southeasterly breeze was holding steady at about fifteen miles an hour. "Let 'er blow," Lafferty commented. "Just what we want." The wind was pushing the main fire into the backfires, just as they'd hoped.

As dusk settled around them and the drama of light and darkness began to unfold, Thomas and Gleeson played the roles of constant watchers and Greek chorus from their post at Powderhouse Turn. Lafferty and Ewing witnessed snatches of the evening's events, but their duties had them involved in operations, running from place to place. Thomas would see disaster in the making and raise the alarm, not once but several times. Gleeson would become eyewitness to the biggest story of his career, a national scoop, and at first he had it alone. Living a newsman's dream inspired him to touches of poetry in his account of the event:

It was still light and a bulldozer crew was silhouetted atop one ridge about a mile away. Flames were burning on three sides, but the road was the fireline. As darkness fell the blaze took on its full beauty in a dozen shades of rose, red, and orange, crawling, reaching out long fingers to catch the tops of digger pines, boiling up in pools that changed colors with each new puff of wind.

Black areas suddenly took on light that turned into acres of jewels. As these burned out they took on the appearance of a city, dazzling with golden lights.

It was 8:10 or 8:15 p.m., a few minutes after Thomas and Gleeson had reached Powderhouse Turn, when an evening breeze started up, blowing an occasional cluster of flaming brush over Alder Springs Road into the canyon below, where there were no containment lines. The fire wasn't going to lie down and die after all. The firefighters posted along the road scrambled from one burning bush to another, beating out the new flames. After a few minutes, Thomas, standing at Powderhouse Turn, saw potential trouble: a spot fire was developing about halfway down the slope on the north side of Powderhouse Canyon, across the bottom of the canyon from the road and too far away for the men there to handle it. Thomas had fought more than a hundred big fires in his career and had no qualms about making tactical decisions – especially with Lafferty and Ewing busy elsewhere – or about picking up a shovel himself.

The new spot fire did not appear at this point to be very threatening. "There were three or four of us there," Thomas wrote later, "including one or two from the lumber company and Chick Gleeson and myself. We thought first of going down to the fire ourselves and putting it out. We did pick up some tools and worked our way in a short distance to a point above the fire." With the wind blowing from the southeast, Thomas figured that if the spot fire flared up it "would probably run up the hill to the top of the point and that the best thing to do was to let it do just that." If it reached "the top of the point," he figured, meaning Powderhouse Turn, they could run a fireline down each side of the flames, starting from the Turn, and catch it that way. "So we did not go down to the fire. We went back to the road at Powderhouse Turn and watched events. About this time the southeast wind died down and became more calm and all of the fires started to settle down."

Spot fires still glimmered and sparkled along the down-canyon side of Alder Springs Road. Emergency lights flashed. Men shouted. As firefighters scrambled, hauling hoses and long-handled tools, firelight danced off the men and their equipment. Silvery streams of water arced from the road onto the fires, which shone ever more brightly as the sky and canyon darkened. When water hit the flames, puffs of white smoke shot upward like geysers from a geologic hell. Then a new spot fire would sparkle into being a few yards away, and the sequence would repeat itself. But the situation was coming under control as the wind died.

> "When we saw this fire down in the valley, a little bitty fire, we didn't know there was any danger."

Flames that had reached feet into the air shrank and flattened into low, pulsing beds of fire.

It must have been quite the mesmerizing sight for anyone with time to stand and watch: silhouetted firefighters battled flames that danced and died in parody of war, and no one got hurt. An hour ticked by. The distant light of day slowly extinguished itself, as though the houselights in a theater were being dimmed in anticipation of the main feature.

Lafferty and Ewing checked in at Powderhouse Turn, and Thomas drew their attention to the untended spot fire on the north side of the canyon. It had not grown since Thomas had first seen it, but it continued to sputter.

The wind, meanwhile, had died out completely. All the spot fires that had begun an hour earlier now had been extinguished, except for that one deep down in the canyon. And once again, it looked as though the fire would be under full control in an hour or two. But that final spot fire had to be extinguished, and they would have to fight it where it was after all. As Lafferty, Ewing, and Thomas talked, four members of the mission crew appeared at Powderhouse Turn and asked for a new assignment; they'd finished their work along the crest of Rattlesnake Ridge, they reported. Lafferty recognized one of the men, David Johnson, as an experienced firefighter. Johnson had attended fireguard school that spring and had fought fire for several seasons before that on the Klamath National Forest. Johnson and his companions became the first of three contingents of firefighters to be sent down to the spot fire, which came to be called the Missionary Spot Fire. Lafferty extracted a promise from Johnson to not "take any undue chances," and Johnson replied that he'd be "careful and cautious."

Missionary Spot Fire

"When we saw this fire down in the valley, just a little bitty fire," remembers Stous, one of the men with Johnson, "we didn't know there was any danger." The fire covered no more than an acre then, when Johnson, Stous, and the other men started down the slope toward it.

It was burning just down from the crest of a smaller spur ridge – one of many – that extended down from the top of the ridge into Powderhouse Canyon.

It was on the back side or down-gulch side of the spur ridge, about 150 yards above the bottom of the canyon, which made it nearly impossible to see from Powderhouse Turn.

Much of the entire canyon, actually, is difficult to see from other locations in the canyon; it's deceptively ridged with gullies and rolling spurs that are far more difficult to negotiate than what they seem from the top or from the road.

Once the missionary crew got to the spot fire, the spur ridge blocked them from seeing back up to the turn. These poor sight lines helped bring on disaster.

Four missionaries were too few to handle the acre-sized blaze. The slope was much steeper than it looked from above, and the dense brush was rubbery-tough and miserable to chop through. Digging was a backbreaker, with hardpan just a few inches below the surface.

"We weren't doing too good and Charlie sent more guys down there," Stous said.

When a second larger batch of missionaries – fifteen this time – showed up at Powderhouse Turn, also finished with their work on the crest of Rattlesnake Ridge and looking for a new assignment, it seemed natural to send them to join their fellow missionaries as reinforcements. Another experienced firefighter, Stanley Vote, led this group. Before dispatching them, Lafferty made certain they had headlamps. As he recounted in hindsight, he told Vote to be "very careful and watch for any change of weather and be sure he had his escape planned." Lafferty was known as an experienced and careful man, by all accounts, and he almost surely said something of the sort.

The time was about 9:30 p.m. and there was still light in the sky, July 9 being one of the longest days of the year, as the fifteen missionaries trekked off Powderhouse Turn and disappeared into the chaparral. A hush fell over the canyon, a quiet that the official report calls "a definite lull." It was truly the calm before the storm.

"The fire was just about out, it was fizzling," remembers Werner. He had tried to get a backfire going along his section of line, the one running up from Powderhouse Turn to High Point in front of the main fire, but without wind to push it his backfire refused to burn. Werner gave up and joined the trickle of firefighters drifting toward the magnet of men and machines collected at Powderhouse Turn.

Powers, too, headed off the same fireline and hiked down to the rally point. Upon arrival there, he discovered that the firefighters sent to the Missionary Spot Fire – a total of nineteen now – had not been fed; one of them had complained before leaving about not having eaten anything since his arrival on the fire.

With nothing else to occupy him, Powers offered to collect sandwiches from the candy wagon parked at Powderhouse Turn and pack them down to the missionary crew. Powers, a man of generous spirit, had a way of making the best of bad circumstances. He had been shot down in Southeast Asia, over Hanoi, during World War II while on an unlucky thirteenth mission as a navigator on a B-24 bomber. Based in China, he was part of the now almost-forgotten Southeast Asian front. He was captured by the Japanese, then beaten and denied medical treatment while in a prisoner-of-war camp. Afterward, he shrugged off the experience, which had left many others dead or embittered for life. "What's there to be bitter about?" he remarked in an interview after his release. "Life was never so good as it is now." Powers had been assigned to the Forest Service station at Alder Springs a few weeks earlier, in May, along with his wife Maude and their children, Bob and Sue.

At the time Powers offered to haul the meals, the Missionary Spot Fire had become nearly invisible to those at Powderhouse Turn: only an occasional flicker was noted. Four more missionaries lingering at the turn without assignment volunteered to help Powers with the food, probably more than were necessary and probably because they, like Powers, took pleasure in being of service. Every one of the twenty-four men who scrambled down to the Missionary Spot Fire volunteered for the assignment.

Lafferty, who had other problems demanding his attention, made sure that Powers and the others had headlamps and then sent them on their way. With the fire dying down, Bill Landrup, the owner of Taylor and Landrup Logging Company, was asking when his men and heavy equipment would be released.

And then the world turned.

One minute the wind was nonexistent, the fire was on its way to extinction, and volunteers were asking to be relieved; in the next minute, the wind sprang to life and so did the fire. Everything changed. The fresh wind, laden with oxygen, struck flames, which shot up and began to boil. Hissing coils of firelight overcame darkness and disclosed the writhing, grotesque shapes of a living nightmare, written in dark shadows and bright flames.

FIRE WEATHER

FOEHN WINDS : Tony Duprey

Wind is the primary driver of wildfire. Without wind, wildfire normally follows topography, burning uphill 18 times faster than on flat ground, depending on steepness of slope. This is because of the preheating of the fuels resulting from heat rising or convection. Without wind, wildfire normally "backs" downhill in a predictable fashion. Wind will overcome topography, though, and push fire downhill at incredible rates of spread.

This is evidenced by worldwide documented "Foehn" winds (or Föhn winds), such as the southern California Santa Ana winds, which normally occur from Santa Barbara County south down the entire Baja Peninsula. Foehn winds are warm, dry winds that blow down the lee (downwind) side of a mountain. Foehn are found worldwide and called by dozens of local names. These winds further dry the area fuels because of the low relative humidity of the air mass as it passes and pre-heats fuels via convection. Such winds can increase the local temperatures by 25 degrees in just a few minutes.

While wind is a component of weather, topographic features such as saddles, canyons, and passes tend to funnel and accelerate already warm, dry Foehn winds – sometimes increasing their velocity to hurricane levels. This same funneling and accelerating action can occur with any type of winds, including normal topographic air subsidence, frontal passage winds, and local-phenomenon winds.

When these winds drive wildfire, resistance to control greatly increases, usually causing firefighters to adopt defensive measures until the fire slows enough, stops, or runs out of fuel, allowing the firefighters to once again assume offensive firefighting strategy and tactics. Once the wind subsides, "normal" fire behavior returns, so a fire that was running with the wind downhill will turn around and burn back uphill at its "normal" high rates of spread.

The Mendocino Front is known for such a local-phenomenon wind. This wind flows from west to east down into the canyons where the Rattlesnake Fire burned.

Tony Duprey, February 2018
Air Tactical Group Supervisor (ATGS)
Chumash Fire Department, Santa Ynez CA

WEATHER 07/09/53 : Chris Cuoco

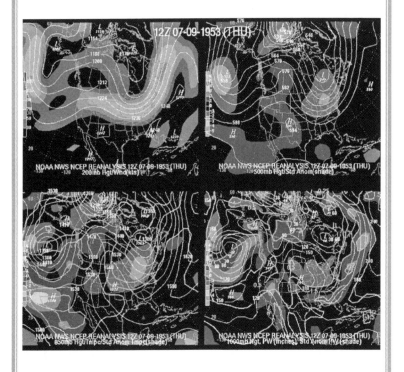

This is a "modernized reanalysis" of four images of 1953 weather data; the strong low pressure system is visible off the west coast. The top right image is 500 mb (millibars) or about 18,000 feet above sea level. The bottom left image is 850 mb (5000 feet above sea level) and the bottom right is at 1000 mb, approximately sea level. Powderhouse Turn is at about 1400 feet, and the ridges of the canyon about 2000 feet elevation.

The Rattlesnake weather was caused by enhanced flow between the high pressure off the coast and the "thermal trough" or heat low stretching across interior California north through Oregon and southwest Idaho. Neither feature is extraordinary. The high off the coast was shallow, and the thermal low was a bit stronger than normal ... this was actually a sundowner in reverse.

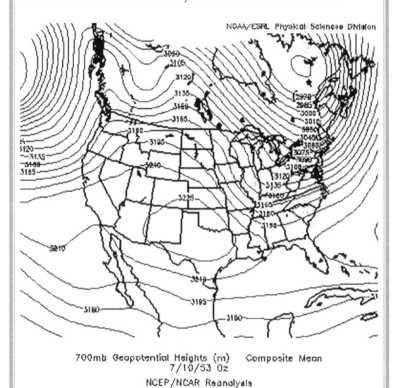

700mb Geopotential Heights (m)   Composite Mean
7/10/53 0z
NCEP/NCAR Reanalysis

This contour map for 7/10 0Z is at 4 p.m. PDT on 7/9. The shallow high pressure off the coast isn't shown and neither is the thermal low (both relatively weak). What is shown is a very strong low pressure system moving into the Gulf of Alaska and what appears to be a shortwave trough that sounded the bottom of that trough and is moving over the northern CA and southern OR coasts. Those 3 or 4 lines close together over northern CA show stronger winds (maybe 25-35 mph) at about 8000 feet above sea level. Those winds could have strengthened the downslope winds that pushed through the gaps and into the valleys involved here.

Chris Cuoco, April 2018
Fire Weather Program Leader
NWS Grand Junction, CO

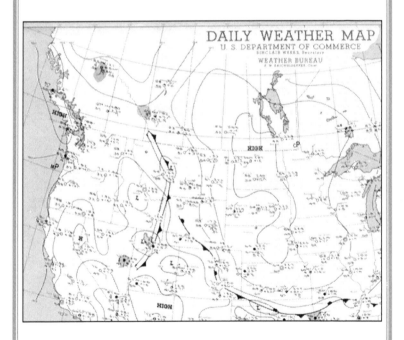

"EVER HEAR A FIRE EXPLODE?"

THE LULL OF EARLY EVENING ENDED at about 10 p.m. when the wind returned, but no longer was it the gentle southeast breeze that had earlier encouraged the firefighters; no longer did it nudge and worry the main fire and the creeping backfires together. The 10 p.m. wind reversed the earlier track by 180 degrees, as contrary as possible, and blew from the northwest, picking up strength and pushing a new crop of bright embers down and over the bank of Alder Springs Road into the canyon below.

This was no ordinary evening breeze, or even a normal "sundowner," coasting down a mountainside as temperatures cooled. A heavy northwest wind now blew unobstructed from the crest of the Coast Range, down the long, steep funnel of Grindstone Canyon, past Long Point Lookout, and on to Powderhouse Canyon. The rushing air became compressed at the narrow V at the head of that canyon and in a *Venturi* effect, gaining momentum by constriction, torrented unabated down into the canyon.

The first heavy puffs of wind fanned old embers to life. Wispy clusters of flaming brush swirled aloft in the darkened sky and rolled spinning cartwheels of flame down over Alder Springs Road. The watchers at Powderhouse Turn could see every stage of the fire's wind-driven advance. "Within a very few minutes there were two or three little spot fires that developed immediately below the road and got no more than twenty-five yards or so from Powderhouse Turn," Thomas recalls.

Lafferty remembers "a sudden change and the fire livened right up."

Flames and shadows once again made grotesquely antic figures of fire trucks, dozers, and firefighters. Again shouts arose, and again men dragged hoses and sent cascading streams of water into the canyon, glittering with the reflections of yellow, orange, and red flames.

"I think we can get it," Thomas told Gleeson.

This time, though, the wind did not die out. This time it erupted.

"I've seen this kind of wind change in southern California but never up here," a worried Thomas told Gleeson. "Ever hear a fire explode? Well, watch this one."

A blowup on a wildfire is an unforgettable event, comparable in violence to a hurricane, a volcanic eruption, or flash flood; it's one of nature's most volatile and destructive phenomena. In the dry terms of fire science, a blowup is nothing more than a sudden increase in fire intensity strong enough "to prevent direct control or upset plans," according to a standard glossary of fire terms. But a true blowup is worthy of legend: a swift, thunderous event engulfing everything in its path in a tidal wave of fire, crimson, orange, and at its most intense white-hot. A blowup occurs when a fire is hit by a sudden massive injection of oxygen from a fresh wind and then explodes into a whirlwind ball of flame, consuming everything from ground litter to the tops of forest giants. The effect is greatly magnified by slope, and a blowup is most intense when confined to a narrow, steep canyon. As long as no one is standing in its way, a blowup is a natural event, occurring many times each year during fire season. Put people in front of it and it becomes the stuff of tragedy.

BLOWUPS ARE COMMON ENOUGH that they were familiar to the secretary of the Glenn County grand jury, Earl Vail. After the fire, during testimony on Pattan's arson case, he asked Lafferty whether a blowup had occurred on the Rattlesnake Fire.

"Charlie, was there an explosion when the fires came together, like there generally is?" Vail asked. "Could you hear it?"

Remarkably Lafferty said, groping, "I imagine there was."

By the time the Rattlesnake Fire blew up, matters more pressing than the sound of the fire preoccupied Lafferty.

As the fresh rash of spot fires along Alder Springs Road were battled and came under some control here and there, Thomas saw tips of flames fingering up from near the bottom of the canyon behind a spur ridge, just as the Missionary Spot Fire had started to do before. This new spot fire, too, had grown unnoticed. But this one was lower in the canyon than the Missionary Spot Fire, way down toward the bottom and well below the log-carved chute beneath Powderhouse Turn. By the time Thomas noticed this spot fire, it had grown to an alarming size.

By Gleeson's later calculation, a quarter hour passed between the time new spot fires ignited along Alder

Springs Road at about 10 p.m., and the time that Thomas noticed the big spot fire in the lower reaches of the canyon. During those fifteen minutes, no one gave a thought to the twenty-four men on the Missionary Spot Fire. There wasn't much to remind anyone: it seemed nothing remained of the Missionary Spot Fire except a few embers. The crew had turned on their headlamps, but the men were hidden away in an isolated spot, tucked behind the spur ridge and out of sight from Powderhouse Turn. The collective amnesia would haunt Lafferty and others.

During this time, the freshened spot fire toward the bottom of the canyon began to make an uphill run on a course straight for Powderhouse Turn. The log chute, because the logs had scoured it somewhat free of brush, made a natural fire barrier, but it needed clearing and especially widening if it was to stop the uphill progress of the spot fire. Bulldozer operators who were asked to perform the job simply refused the assignment; the slopes were too steep for the dozers, they argued. CDF firefighters who toured the site fifty years later agreed with that judgment. "Easy to get in, hard to get out" was the wisdom of hindsight. But that did not stop the refusal from becoming a public and nasty controversy directly after the fire.

> No one gave a thought to the twenty-four men on the Missionary Spot Fire.

The log chute, nonetheless, had to be cleared by somebody. A fire truck was backed to the head of the chute, and two men started down the side of the canyon, one unrolling a fire hose from the truck and the other wielding a flaming torch. The plan was for them to drop down and burn out a little V on the side of the canyon, as Thomas later described it, the sharp point of the V lowest down and the sides of the V expanding on the existing chute. As the two men descended, the man with the torch began burning one side of the chute, while the other used the hose to control the flames.

From down in the canyon, looking up toward the site of the Missionary Spot Fire with the lunch spot at right and log chute at left.

Once the men worked their way to the bottom of the chute, they were to start back up the other side and do the same thing, firing along the way, thus creating a scorched V broad enough to block the spot fire's upward progress. The scheme nearly got both men killed. The spot fire unexpectedly picked up speed and came roaring up the slope, threatening to cut off the men's retreat and burn over them. They instantly abandoned the firing operation and started a mad scramble back up to the road. The footing was loose and the slope nearly sheer. The shale came away when they grabbed it. With inspiration born of desperation, they had the crazy idea to climb up the fire hose, and it worked. They grappled their way upward, hand over hand, climbing for their lives. The hose was stout and firmly attached to the truck, and it held. The men spurted out of the canyon with flames on their heels, and inspired the false rumor, which exists to this day, that it was men from the Missionary Spot Fire who had climbed the fire hose to safety.

The new spot fire's threat to Powderhouse Turn, though, had one good result: it at last triggered fears for those twenty-four men tucked away out of sight down on the Missionary Spot Fire.

"It was then that several of us realized the possibility of the spot fire jumping the log chute and burning in the direction of the low saddle on Powderhouse Turn," Thomas recalls. "And there were several of us that mentioned the necessity of warning these people here if they had not already known about it."

Thomas' description sounds like a good bureaucrat writing a dull report. What actually happened was a terrified realization of life-threatening danger by the men who had put the missionary crew in harm's way, instantly followed by a near panic.

"Has anyone warned the missions, the boys on the spot?" Thomas asked.

Without a word in response, Lafferty took off at a dead run. He sprinted up the road toward Powderhouse Ridge and onto the dozer line that had been cut along the top earlier in the day. He ran along the dozer fireline until he could see headlamps below him from the Missionary Spot Fire crew; he then dropped down into the heavy brush, plowing down toward them.

"I started calling to the boys to get out. I yelled, 'Get out, hurry out!' and went down the ridge as I was calling them."

Farther downhill, below the lights of the crew's headlamps, Lafferty could see cherry-red flames lunging upward.

"The fire was rolling toward me at, I would say, a very fast clip," Lafferty recalled. "And I noticed the lights were spreading. And some lights coming up toward – to the ridge." He recalled hearing a "terrific roar" at this time, though not exactly an explosion.

"And then the lights just came on with terrific force, like a – numerous floodlights from the main fire, coming at me. The light from the sky was illuminating the whole thing for me." Truly, some men saw the event unfold on one mental level as though it actually were a staged drama and not a real-time disaster.

Waves of heat buffeted Lafferty.

He shouted again, this time telling everyone to go *downhill*, not up toward him. It was the only safe place he could see for them to escape. *Fires never burned downhill*, and this one, true to experience, was burning uphill, toward the crew and Lafferty. He waved and shouted over and over, "Go downhill, downhill!"

The headlamps, which at first were formed up in a stationary circle, began to swirl in alarmed confusion as Lafferty yelled. After a few moments, as Lafferty continued to shout for the men to go downhill, the headlamps divided into two groups: fifteen lights strung out in an orderly line and headed down the canyon, following his direction to go downhill; but nine lights, contrary to his order, came straight up the slope toward him. Referring to the group heading downhill, Lafferty would later say in an agony of self-defense, "I feel in my own mind and heart, had the boys tried to make their escape by coming to the top of the ridge they would not, could not, possibly have done so. I felt at the time they were making the best possible route of escape."

The heat became too much for Lafferty.

"I realized I had to leave immediately in order to save my life," Lafferty recalled. He headed straight back to Powderhouse Turn, not retracing his steps up toward the bulldozer line but taking a quicker, more direct sidehill route across the slope and through the brush.

The dense chaparral was impenetrable for an upright man; Lafferty fell to his hands and knees and scurried "like a rabbit would do." The brush tore off his hard hat, but he didn't dare stop to retrieve it. Thorny branches whipped his face and bare head. The shale cut his hands and knees. Once he cleared the brush, he ran as hard as his legs would take him to report to Thomas at Powderhouse Turn. "By golly, we made it!" he gushed.

He'd broken free of the brush at last, but it was a temporary reprieve, not real freedom. The man would wander Alder Springs Road like a lost soul for the rest of the night, begging others to give him hope for the men of the missionary crew.

"I SAW THE DOOMED MEN'S LIGHTS."

IT WAS LATE, PAST 10 P.M., when Powers reached the missionary crew with their suppers. The men had cut a line around their spot fire, which burned in heavy brush, and they'd contained it. When Powers arrived, they were tired and hungry, and they sat down in a circle to eat, rather than walking up and out of the canyon. They were in tall chaparral, on the lee side of the fire, and had no view of the fire's sudden and unexpected moves that began around this time. They picked a peaceful spot for supper, on the low down-canyon side of their spot fire, now contained, and they seated themselves in a circle for fellowship. The brush around them was so tall that they could not see out even when they stood up. But they set no lookouts. Vote and Powers talked about lookouts, survivors would recall, but with the Missionary Spot Fire virtually dead out, they thought they were perfectly safe: the main fire, with its active flames, was on the opposite side of the canyon, and above the road, far from them. Darkness was everywhere around them.

Their foreman, Stanley Vote, had just said a short grace and they were taking the first bites of their sandwiches when they heard Lafferty yelling at them from above. His first shouts were unintelligible. Schlatter, the Indiana schoolteacher, could not make out what Lafferty said, but he got to his feet with the others and began walking uphill. "My understanding at the time was that the rangers on the hill were calling us to come up to them, and I assumed they had other responsibilities for us," Schlatter recalls. "I don't remember being in a panic or extremely fearful, because I had not heard the details of what was apparently said." Jack Toews, another missionary, said he assumed they were being sent to another fire. "I just stuck my sandwich back in the pack and grabbed my tools and started up the hill," Toews said.

Some of the men were alarmed and hurried, however, and dropped their tools. Schlatter stopped to pick them up.

As the missionaries started the climb, Dinnel was directly in front of Schlatter, but after a few steps Dinnel unaccountably veered down the canyon, joining the party heading that way. Perhaps he heard Lafferty yelling to go downhill; perhaps he was trying to get out of the path of the fire coming up from below. Schlatter had walked out in that direction earlier, the down-canyon side of the spur ridge, and he remembered that brush as exceptionally thick. That route was not for him; he continued straight up.

He never saw Dinnel again.

"When I got to the top I expected to find the other fellows up there, too, and was surprised that so few of us were at the top of the ridge," Schlatter remembered.

Emerging from the brush behind Schlatter were Stous and Ken Etherton, who was the mission dentist. Stous had started out in the lead but had turned back when Etherton began to struggle.

"Charlie hollered down to us, 'Get out of there!'" remembered Stous, "and we took off up the side of the mountain. It was pretty steep; the manzanita was shoulder-high. I wasn't scared. I just happened to be in the lead. We got about halfway up when Charlie called, 'You're not going to make it! Run down, run away from the fire.' I looked down and thought, *That's stupid. I'm not going to run back down there.* I don't think the other guys would have made it, anyway; some of them may have been slow pulling their stuff together. And we didn't realize the danger. We never could see the fire until later."

A few yards behind Stous, Etherton fell to his knees. He collapsed in utter exhaustion, and told Stous to keep going, to save himself. "I was nearly dead," said Etherton later. "I couldn't have gone a step farther." Stous urged him back to his feet.

"Ken was totally out of shape," Stous remembered. "I was in excellent shape, real athletic. About halfway up Ken was absolutely petered out. He said, 'I've got to rest, I'm going to lie down.' I just kept after him, encouraging him, helping him along. He hit that firebreak and was sick the rest of the night from exhaustion."

Ahead of Stous and Etherton, Toews and several others began to race upward toward the firebreak, dropping their tools as they ran. "We began to feel the heat from the flames and boy, I almost lost all my strength and I started to get kind of frantic," Toews said. "Someone ahead of me dropped their shovel. Some of the other boys picked it up. Then a canteen, then I saw a coat. And then we just kept moving. When we reached the top, we just got up there and laid down."

When the nine missionaries reached the bulldozer firebreak, though, they were still in danger. The other spot fire, which had crossed the log chute by then, threatened to run up the ridge ahead of them and cut off their retreat back to Powderhouse Turn. It looked as though the fire would sweep the bulldozer line and even Powderhouse Turn itself, and burn over the top into Grindstone Canyon. The men at Powderhouse Turn had many options for retreat, but the nine missionaries could be caught long before they got there.

> "We began to feel the heat from the flames and boy, I almost lost all my strength and I started to get kind of frantic. Someone ahead of me dropped their shovel. Some of the other boys picked it up. Then a canteen, then I saw a coat. And then we just kept moving."

At this point, Ewing, the fire boss who had forgotten a crew and lost eleven men on the Hauser Creek Fire, had a bit of redemption.. He ran hard from Powderhouse Turn toward the flames and the nine struggling missionaries, hollering at them to keep coming along the bulldozer line, out to Powderhouse Turn. The men followed his urgings and escaped, stumbling into the turn like souls escaping purgatory: ashen-faced, goggle-eyed, and shaking like leaves. But they gave morale there a big boost.

"When I saw the nine men come out, at first I did not really think it was them," Thomas recalled. "I heaved a sigh of relief because I figured that was all there were – the boys got out."

The situation at this point was dangerous but recoverable. Grindstone Canyon might well burn out, a spectacular embarrassment to the Forest Service and its policy of suppressing all fires on sight. But no one had been seriously injured. The nine missionaries were safe, thanks to fast and courageous action by Lafferty and Ewing. The fifteen others were headed in what seemed the safest direction, down the canyon and away from the flames.

At this time, between 10:20 and 10:30 p.m., the wind changed direction so suddenly and with such violence that it bewildered veterans of many a nighttime battle with fire. Winds normally switch direction after dark, changing from uphill currents, caused by land heating during the day, to downhill currents, as the land cools and draws the air downward. This radiation effect was well known in 1953, and it explains the initial downdrafts on the Rattlesnake Fire.

Nighttime winds, however, normally do not cause blowups. They do not send fire crashing down canyons. They are not killers. Nighttime fires tend to be slow-moving "creepers." Temperatures are cooler, the humidity is higher, and winds generally are more moderate. The explanation for the dramatic wind shift on the Rattlesnake Fire would be a while in coming. No weather observations were taken at Powderhouse Canyon the night of the fire, but meteorologists were sent to the site the next two nights, and their observations provided the raw data for a theory about the cause of the fatal downdraft, an explanation that has stood the test of time.

But on the evening of July 9 no one understood what was happening. The wind action seemed to defy both science and firefighter experience. An enormous mass of air swept without warning over the lip of Powderhouse Canyon, as though a dam had burst and loosed an unstoppable torrent. Flames turned from cherry red to intense yellow and incandescent white. Embers showered into the lowest reaches of the canyon, raining down to ignite new spot fires, which melded into the existing fires, multiplying in power many times over. The flames leaped a hundred yards and more on the wings of the spinning embers.

Perversely, the fire burned downhill faster than firefighters had ever seen flames go *uphill*. Powderhouse Canyon morphed into a raging nighttime inferno. It flouted the common wisdom about fire intensity, which is that fires move fastest and burn hottest when traveling uphill during the day, driven by sun and slope.

The sight rattled Gleeson, who wrote a jittery but vivid description of it. "By now the entire canyon was a sparkling mass of red jewels, sparking in the night wind, as you looked down from your secure spot along the point where you knew nothing could live more than a few moments in that inferno."

Thomas would be struggling weeks later to paint a coherent word picture: "The wind suddenly shifted and came up the 'V' slope, in a northwesterly direction," he told the Glenn County grand jury, describing the initial fire movement that drove the missionaries up the side of the ridge. "The whole side of that fire [the downhill flank of the fire] then became a front, and it was just a matter of minutes until the whole thing just swept right down the canyon. In other words, the whole smoke and everything just laid down. And from that time on, it just burned very rapidly down the whole canyon."

For the men on the Alder Springs Road, the fire was more than an engaging spectacle: it now directly threatened them. Flames blasted across the road, bubbling and scorching the paint on their trucks. The youngster Pesonen found himself alone with the Power Wagon near Powderhouse Turn; Silva was off on another assignment. As flames licked at the truck, Pesonen asked someone what to do. Use your hose, he was told.

"I sprayed myself and the fire truck – all of us were doing that – while the fire leaned over the road," Pesonen remembered decades later, standing in the same place where it had happened, on Alder Springs Road. "It didn't take long before someone said, 'There's a bunch of people down there.' I hadn't seen them go down there ... but I had a feeling."

Werner watched from Powderhouse Turn as flames came to life along the fireline he had walked away from minutes before, the one that ran up from Powderhouse Turn to High Point on the ridge to the south. A tongue of fire darted downhill from High Point and threatened the turn. Werner grabbed a hose and ran toward the flames, shooting a jet of water. He quenched that run of fire and turned to look for others.

Behind him, on the opposite slope of the canyon, he saw a circle of tiny lights, each burning with equal intensity, an image that had to be of human design, not nature's random work. The circle of lights broke apart and fewer than half them headed up the side of the canyon, some haltingly, some quick as squirrels, with the fire chasing right behind them.

The fire hesitated as if taking a deep breath.

"You could see it coming," Werner asserted. And in seconds the "it" arrived, a mighty wind that turned the fire ninety degrees and sent it plunging down the canyon, now chasing the larger group of lights, little lights that moved single file down into the dark depths of the canyon.

The change was so decisive that flames that had been racing uphill fast enough to nearly overtake Lafferty and the nine others – Lafferty was sure those farthest back in this group couldn't make it out – instead took more than a half hour to creep the last hundred yards to the top of Rattlesnake Ridge, edging up the slope, nibbling through brush against the downslope wind. In less than half that time, maybe twenty minutes, the main fire heading downhill ripped for more than a mile, tearing down the entire length of Powderhouse Canyon to its mouth.

Moments later, when Lafferty staggered back up to Powderhouse Turn, all he knew was that the fire had been chasing him and some men behind him. Werner overheard Lafferty say that nobody behind him was going to make it up; he had ordered them to head down the canyon, the only safe direction.

"And he was right," Werner said – as long as the fire continued uphill.

Headlamps appeared at Powderhouse Turn, coming along behind Lafferty. "I was standing right there, not over a hundred yards from where they come up, and I counted them and there was nine," Werner said. "The fire at this point was howling. I can't quite describe what it sounded like, like Niagara Falls, and making an awful lot of noise."

Near the fork just above the Gillaspy ranch, with Alder Springs Road visible up the canyon in the center.

Powderhouse Canyon from its lower reaches.

Curiously, others too remembered the wind and fire as the rush of a watery torrent. Pesonen even described it as "a heavy rain."

Then a sound came on the wind, a curious siren wail too sweet for a scream, not desperate enough for a yell. It sounded to Werner like singing voices. Werner asked one of the missionaries standing nearby, "Did you hear that?"

"Yes," the man replied.

The singing sound went on for two or three minutes – what seemed then an eternity. Perhaps more men had escaped and were singing in jubilation, Werner thought; perhaps it was nothing more than the alarm of a backing truck. He started to run along the road looking for survivors, and he quickly met a missionary on the same errand.

"Did you see anything?" Werner asked.

"No, they're not down there," the man replied.

By the time Werner returned to Powderhouse Turn, the singing sound had stopped, never to resume, and never to be explained. Nature was dislocated; nothing was as it should be. Fires became watery torrents, raged downhill, and sang songs about it.

Powderhouse Canyon is a natural amphitheater, with Alder Springs Road forming a virtual gallery along one side. The canyon has a narrow head, a slot in the shape of a V, at Powderhouse Turn. Below that, the canyon widens some as it funnels out, but it remains remarkably narrow and steep along its entire mile and a half length, until it fans out broadly just above the Gillaspy ranch.

The sides of the canyon undulate with deceptively steep spur ridges; no one who did not have to would walk such a treacherous place. The roller-coaster terrain means a hiker would cover much more than a mile and a half going from one end to the other. Adding to the difficulties, the canyon is blanketed now, as it was then, by unbroken chaparral waist-high to head-high or higher. One and only one outstanding feature marks its entire length: a knobby outcropping of rock, which came to be called Missionary Rock, about a quarter mile as the crow flies below Powderhouse Turn, on the north slope opposite Alder Springs Road.

As events unfolded, Powderhouse Turn became a commanding box seat over a stage set for tragic drama. A common characteristic of fatal wildfires is an absence of witnesses to the final act. There are sometimes spectators during the early parts of a race with wildfire, but the last minutes, virtually by definition, are hidden from sight in a fury of smoke and flame.

The final tragic act of the Rattlesnake Fire, however, played out before a stunned and horrified audience, fully aware of the likely end to the drama and utterly incapable of stopping it. Darkness was no mercy. Instead, nightfall turned the last act into a living theater of lights and shadows, complete with sound and motion. The human characters played their roles as pinpoints of light – the headlamps of firefighters – sometimes stationary, sometimes scrambling, sometimes lined out in purposeful moving formation.

> The sides of the canyon undulate with deceptively steep spur ridges; no one who did not have to would walk such a treacherous place.

The fire wore many masks. It started out on more or less equal terms with the humans, like them as

113

pinpoints of light, namely the spot fires that wavered, winked, and mostly snuffed out along the canyon wall below Alder Springs Road. Then a new spot fire, deeper in the canyon than any other, deeper by far than the Missionary Spot Fire on the spur ridge, appeared and quickly transformed itself into a climbing wall of cherry-red flame; it took off after a handful of the tiny bobbing human lights, the headlamps of nine men of the mission crew scrambling to get out of the canyon and the path of the fire by climbing straight up the canyon's far side.

The fire below them grew from a little spot into a mounting wave of flame, headed up the side of Powderhouse Canyon directly after them. It was about to overtake those headlamps when for a second time everything changed, in defiance of common sense and experience or any notion of divine or human justice, mercy, or fair play.

In a moment of diabolical contrariness the flames, terrible enough in themselves, transformed from an ascending wave into a swirling, spinning cauldron of fire. A gale wind tipped – and then poured over the lip of Powderhouse Canyon, seeming to come from nowhere, whipping the fire into a writhing frenzy. The cauldron of fire near the top then tipped and *poured its flames down the canyon,* changing the direction of this part of the fire ninety degrees and thus abandoning the chase it had been about to win against the nine headlamps.

Denying the principle that fire will race uphill but not down, the boiling mass of fire roared downward, dead on the heels of a second and even larger batch of headlamps – the fifteen remaining members of the missionary crew, who until that moment had been bobbing along in single file on a down-canyon path of supposed escape. Suddenly the fifteen headlamps had nowhere safe to go. The canyon below them was deep, tortuous, and seemingly endless. The slopes on either side, above and below, were long and steep. Behind them a wave of flame lunged toward them in an arcing, rolling wave of destruction. The drama of lights, of flames thundering down the canyon in pursuit of the tiny, all-too-human headlamps, etched its way forever into the minds of the men who stood by helplessly and watched it happen.

HANCOCK, WHO'D DRIVEN THE MISSION CREW transport, found himself halfway down Alder Springs Road with his truck blocked by the fire. Flames licked into the truck's cab and scorched the seat.

"Never have I seen a fire travel so fast," Hancock said later.

On the opposite slope, a line of lights moved steadily in single file down the canyon. The lights flickered in and out of sight as the men beneath the headlamps followed the dips and rises of the many spur ridges. Behind the lights, the onrushing fire rose in a wave more than one hundred feet high; flames fanned out across the width of the canyon from Powderhouse Ridge to Alder Springs Road. Nothing was to be spared. The fire spumed embers that ignited instant blazes along its path. Bounding, howling flames gained on the headlamps with the ferocity of hellfire.

Hancock watched, transfixed.

"It was evident that there was no chance of escape for all of those who were headed down, as the flames were jumping forward at an unbelievable rate of speed, more like an explosion than the normal travel of fire," he said.

On the slope heading up to the rocky outcropping, later called Missionary Rock, the fire caught up with and washed over the headlamp farthest back in the line. The little light disappeared under a tidal wave of flame. Without a pause, the flames obliterated another headlamp. At this point, some of the remaining headlamps broke out of line and scattered in several directions. One lonely light struck out on its own for the crest of Powderhouse Ridge, hundreds of yards above. A second broke in the opposite direction, down toward the bottom of Powderhouse Canyon. This second light made it all the way down the steep canyon wall, across the narrow bottom, and up the opposite slope nearly to Alder Springs Road. It traveled farther, lasted longer, and came closer to escape than any other, but at last it was in turn overcome.

Most of the lights remained together, but the farther they went, the closer they got to a sheer drop-off, a ravine steeper than any they had encountered so far. As the lights neared the drop-off, they collapsed in a heap on themselves.

"I saw the doomed men's lights," Hancock later recounted. "Suddenly there were flames behind them, then a puff of smoke. I actually saw the flames envelop the lights and go over their heads and then all I could see was smoke, and then all was black." A forest official asked Hancock afterward, "When the flames swept over the men did you hear any sound?" He replied, "Yes. We did hear one shrill scream."

The heat drove back most of the men along Alder Springs Road, but not Hancock. He held his ground next to his scorched truck. After the fire had passed, the others drifted back and asked him for news. Swirling dust, soot, and ashes made it difficult to see into the canyon. Hancock said what he could.

"The boys are down there. The boys are down in that fire."

"I COULDN'T SEE ANY BODIES, BUT THEY WERE THERE."

THE FIRE LEFT IN ITS WAKE a bed of pulsing red and yellow embers. "We were all very anxious about what had happened," Thomas said. "The whole canyon at this time was just a mass of hot smoldering embers and snag and brush fire, just a mass of red glow." The scene reminded one firefighter of a lighted city at night, a city that had been bombed out and evacuated: the embers were the only sign of life. Lafferty radioed Hancock and asked whether any of the lost crew had shown up near him. No, Hancock replied, he had seen no one.

The embers sent up waves of heat that made it impossible for many hours for anyone to venture into the canyon. Until that could happen, Lafferty detailed men and trucks to patrol the road for survivors. Worried about the continuing threat to massive Grindstone Canyon, he remembered that a side road from Powderhouse Turn to the dynamite shed on the far north side of Powderhouse Ridge continued downhill, circled back, and connected to Alder Springs Road below the mouth of the canyon. The road might make a good firebreak. Using it as a base to backfire the top of Powderhouse Ridge could create a buffer to contain the northern edge of the fire and protect Grindstone Canyon.

Lafferty sent a bulldozer, a water tanker, and a crew to clear the side road, which was overgrown with brush.

He delayed the firing operation until the lost crew had had every chance to escape. The backfiring operation commenced about midnight and was a success: Grindstone Canyon was spared.

Pesonen and his Power Wagon were among those assigned to overnight patrol duty. "It was quite an initiation for me," Pesonen said later. At one point, two missionaries stumbled into the beams of his headlamps as he patrolled near the dynamite shed, and he hit the brakes. "They were exhausted and almost hysterical," Pesonen remembers. They must have just escaped the flames, he thought; a Jeep coming along behind him took the men to the fire camp for a much-needed rest.

After patrolling through the night without food or rest, Pesonen decided at daybreak to call it quits. He drove along Alder Springs Road past the remains of the fire, heading for fire camp. The first rays of daylight illuminated a grim, gray panorama over the canyon and ridges. "I couldn't see any bodies in the ashes, but they were there," he remembered. "I began to hear over the radio that people on foot had discovered the bodies."

Touring the site decades later, Pesonen still thought the two men had run out of the fire, directly into the glare of his headlights. But the nine survivors had made their escape hours before this happened, and no one else made it out. Today, firefighters who have a close call are whisked away for a stress debriefing and offered professional counseling. Not so in 1953. After their escape, the nine surviving missionaries were ordered to help with the backfiring operation. The men in Pesonen's headlights probably were part of this group, which would account for their location on the road and their distraught appearance.[3]

A shout went up at 4:45 a.m., when men with flashlights found the first body. Sheriff Sale and the Glenn County deputy coroner, Howard F. Sweet, had been summoned during the night. With daylight and more hands, by 5:45 a.m. they had located all fifteen bodies – within an hour after finding the first one.

One band of missionaries, meanwhile, had spent the night along the top of Rattlesnake Ridge, dozing fitfully on the ground.

Paul Turner, the missionary who was crew boss for this group, remembered waking up not knowing exactly what had happened the night before. When fire swept the canyon, he and the others said a prayer for the men below. Surely God would watch over and protect his own, Turner thought.

---

[3] "Now there are indeed standing USFS Critical Incident Stress Debriefing (CISD) teams that are on an on-call status," wrote Don Will, explaining the present situation. "This is working very well. The teams are trained and certified and do an absolutely wonderful job of fast mobilization and working with involved personnel." He said the teams mobilize and arrive at the incident location and begin the initial debrief before those involved sleep that day, which is a key to the process.

"A young firefighter was killed on my very first fire in June of 1973 on the Los Padres. The guy fell off a cliff late on the first night and rolled head over heels into Logwood Creek and landed on the rocks. Died right there. Later that same night, I was rolled over by rocks that came bounding down the hill. Smashed my right leg. I limped out the next day on my McLeod. We never received any kind of stress debrief, not in those days. All just part of the job ... just like the nine survivors on the Rattlesnake."

The CISD teams are part of a National Fire & Aviation Critical Incident Stress Management (CISM) program that has many options and can be tailored to a specific incident.

But as he came awake in dawn's half-light, he looked across the canyon and saw a handful of small, intense lights pop and then quickly fade on the opposite slope, in an eerie echo of the previous night's fatal play of headlamps. It took Turner a moment to realize that the lights were flashbulbs. Photos meant serious trouble.

A bit later, a Forest Service ranger found Turner's group, told them what he could about the lost crew, and escorted them off the ridge and back over to Powderhouse Turn, where they had a silent breakfast together at the candy wagon.

> "It was obvious I didn't know anything about God."

The question *Why?* ran and re-ran in Turner's mind. Why had the God of his faith and understanding, a God of goodness and mercy, allowed this horror to occur? The men who died were God's servants, doing His will.

"I had trouble resolving this in my mind," Turner said years later. "The biggest problem I had was understanding how the God that I thought I knew would allow this to happen. These fellas were giving their lives to go out as missionaries and this was something that was close to God's heart; He wouldn't allow it to happen."

Pattan had been free to exercise his will and set the fire, said Turner. But God should have controlled the wind. "Why didn't God intervene, or at least why didn't He control the elements? I have never resolved that dilemma to this day."

Turner, an elder for New Tribes Mission at the time of the fire, began to wonder whether he should continue with missionary work. "It was obvious I didn't know anything about God," he said. "The kind of God I believed in wouldn't let anything like this happen. And I began to talk that way."

Turner was counseled to keep such views to himself, especially considering that he was an elder.

"I told my wife we should just turn around and go back where we came from and forget about missionary work. Once you're into something like this it's difficult to stop, to admit you made a mistake and that you ought to quit. So we went on."

Turner served many years as a missionary in Venezuela and he later taught anthropology at the University of Arizona in Tucson.

Body recovery the day after the fatalities

AS TURNER AND THE OTHERS trudged down from Rattlesnake Ridge, daylight brought to a close the drama of lights and shadows and darkness. The once-dense brush had been replaced by low blackened stobs that formed a broken web pattern, a fisherman's net torn to tatters, on the exposed mineral soil. Thin blankets of smoke drifted over the canyon. Deep shadows filled the ravines until, as the sun rose higher, even the shadows disappeared. The fully lit scene was one of drab, unrelieved gray and black.

"About an hour before daylight the area cooled down to a point where we could put a few qualified men in to look for the missing men," Thomas said later. The men took flashlights and began their search at the site of the Missionary Spot Fire, working their way down into the bottom of the gulch and eventually discovering a body up near Alder Springs Road. They realized they had to search higher up and went back to their start point; from there they roughly followed the same path the fleeing firefighters had followed. As the sky lightened, Sheriff Sale, Deputy Coroner Sweet, and others became visible to the survivors along Alder Springs Road. The search party stood around a cluster of soft horizontal shapes – they could have been gear bags or charred logs piled together. A careful observer, though, would have noted similar bundles nearby, maybe two or three more.

"Some of the bodies could be seen easily from the road about 300 yards across the canyon," wrote Gleeson. "But if you didn't have glasses, you might have taken them for small clumps of dark green brush surrounded by gray ashes."

Hancock and others tried to identify the dead, but the bodies were too badly burned. It took until 8:30 a.m. the next day, July 11, before all the victims were positively identified.

- Allan J. Boddy, 30, married with three children – Salem, Oregon.
- Sergio Colles, 40, married – Lancaster, Pennsylvania.
- Benjamin O. Dinnel, 26, single – Chico, California.
- Paul Gifford, 34, single – Vancouver, British Columbia, Canada.
- Harold Jesse Griffis, 37, married with seven children – North Platte, Nebraska.
- Glenn Cecil Hitchcock, 20, single – Littleton, Colorado.

- David A. Johnson, 27, married with four children – Oakland, California.
- Robert James Mieden, 35, married with two children – Glendale, California.
- Darrel Kent Noah, 31, married with four children – Ogallah, Kansas.
- Robert F. Powers, 35, assistant Forest Service ranger, married with two children – Alder Springs, California.
- Howard Fred Rowe, 25, married with three children – Chicago, Illinois.
- Raymond C. Sherman, 20, married – Seattle, Washington.
- Daniel G. Short, 20, single – Ypsilanti, Michigan.
- Stanley L. Vote, 24, single – Birchdale, Minnesota.
- Hobard S. Whitehouse, 30, married with four children – Denver, Colorado.

The men had fallen far from any road, so a dozer operator cut a trail across the slope to allow emergency vehicles in. Clint Hensley, the operator, kept a searing memory: one body, that of the firefighter who had struck out alone for the top of Powderhouse Ridge, was found with its fingers broken backward, perhaps a heat effect, but more likely from frantic digging.

For Stous, watching from Alder Springs Road, the sight seemed to confirm the judgment of those who had warned him against joining New Tribes Mission. Stous had enrolled in Bible school in Los Angeles a year and a half earlier, after his wife Ladene was killed in an auto accident, leaving him to care for their three children. He'd felt restless in Bible school, however, and before graduating he'd begun to consider joining New Tribes Mission, though friends had cautioned him to avoid the group because of its record of violent deaths. Stous had packed up the children anyway and headed for Fouts Springs, arriving three days before the fire. As he stared at the ruins of Powderhouse Canyon, his dreams seemed to turn to ash.

Dozer work on the fire site. It took most of the day to recover the bodies.

"That morning when I saw those fellas dead, I hit bottom," Stous remembered. "I walked off sick to my stomach. *There is something wrong with this organization,* I thought."

But as he wandered off alone, his thoughts turned to his dead wife, Ladene. He could have been killed in the auto accident with her, but he had lived. He could have been killed the night before in the fire, but once again he had survived. Coming that close to death and escaping twice could not be happenstance. It must have meaning. God must be saving him for a purpose, he thought.

"I've been in this outfit fifty years and I've never doubted since."

Stous, Schlatter, and Etherton were chosen to carry the bad news to Fouts Springs. When the three of them

arrived there, the scene at the mission camp was a terrible one, made worse by some premature radio reports announcing the names of some of the dead. (Similar episodes over the years have led today's fire and police departments, along with professional media, to condemn this practice and agree to a policy of withholding the names of victims until next of kin have been notified. Social media and the internet, however, now can and sometimes do preempt the official release of victims' identities, and the scene at Fouts Springs has since been replayed in other places.)

Stous felt guilty and embarrassed walking through the camp. If only he had died, he thought, a married man might be alive in his place. Because his wife had died a violent death, he understood all too well the suffering he saw around him. At the very least, he could offer the widows his heartfelt sympathy and understanding.

He sought out Mary Rowe, whose husband Howard had befriended him during his few days in camp. Howard had introduced him to Mary and their two children; Mary was pregnant, which would make three for her, a match number with his own three children. Over the next weeks, as Stous prayed for the widows, he found himself praying especially for Mary.

Lingering smoke the day after the fatalities

"I went and talked with her about it and we became friends," Stous said. They married the next year in the spring and bravely took their joined families – six children, all aged six or younger – to a jungle mission in Paraguay, where they remained for the next twelve years and produced a seventh child, Juanita. In semiretirement fifty years after the fire, Stous was teaching part-time at the New Tribes Bible Institute in Waukesha, Wisconsin, when I located him and he told his story. We met in person a few years later, at a memorial gathering to acknowledge the fire.

When Schlatter returned to Fouts Springs, he conferred with the camp director, Macon Hare, and they decided not to pass on what little they knew about the identities of the dead; a truck carrying the survivors was

129

due in camp at any moment, and the fates of the firefighters would become all too clear.

"At that time we weren't sure how many had actually perished," Schlatter said. "Everybody was in shock."

Word spread anyway, and by the time the Forest Service truck arrived, the names of all but one of the victims were known. Turner remembers riding the survivors' truck into the camp and seeing an assembly of women anxiously waiting. He caught sight of his wife and his mother-in-law, who was visiting from Illinois. The three of them embraced, weeping.

Lonesome

"And the other wives were there to meet their husbands, and one of them didn't have a husband coming back," Turner said. "When everyone got off the truck and she realized her husband wasn't coming back, she collapsed."

Schlatter began to serve as a family liaison with the Forest Service and the coroner, taking items found on the bodies and showing them to widows to aid in identification: a bronze fire badge, a metal belt buckle and a gasoline credit card, a swatch of fabric. The men had few possessions to begin with, and very little was left. Grisly as this errand sounds, the act of seeing and touching objects belonging to their husbands somehow brought comfort to the widows, and to Schlatter. "I experienced at that time a distinct sense of God's presence," he said. "That fire was a most tragic event and created terrible suffering, but for those of us who survived it, that event was something very special in our lives."

For Schlatter, the sense of being called to a renewed purpose in life came gradually, not in a rush as it had for Stous. But it was equally strong. Schlatter knew he could have died with the fifteen other men, and he could not explain why his life had been spared. But there had to be a reason, he thought: everything happens for a reason.

"It was God who determined my steps," Schlatter said years later. "That's why I feel God had a purpose in it for me. I was alive only because of God's providence."

A month after the fire, he and his wife left for Thailand, which is where they were still serving as missionaries when I contacted them many decades later. They have two sons, Philip and Tom, and a daughter, Mary, all of whom were born in Thailand and have also become missionaries, plus an adopted daughter, Joanna. Schlatter told me his story in an exchange of emails over a lengthy time period. His remote mission headquarters had no computer link and we corresponded when he occasionally flew to a more urban base. He made only one request: that his views be presented, if at all, in full.

"It was a time in my life that was very sad," he wrote, "and yet I believe it was something that brought a sense of assurance that life does have meaning and purpose, and I trust it has caused me to desire a closer walk with God. The answer has to be not just faith as such, but faith in a God who is truly good. I praise him for his faithfulness through all these years!"

Observers at Fouts Springs that day took away near-psychedelic impressions of the impact of disaster visited upon a deeply religious community. Tim Adams, a reporter for the *San Francisco Chronicle*, was struck by the bleakness of the surroundings: primitive cabins stuck in the heart of brush country. Asking directions of a pretty girl wearing a gingham dress and no makeup, he mentioned the horror of the fire.

The girl smiled.

"God's will is sufficient in all things," responded Gerry Sherman, age twenty-one. She had married one of the victims, Raymond Sherman, just five weeks earlier; the couple had come to Fouts Springs just a few days before the fire. When word of the disaster first trickled back to the camp, Mrs. Sherman told the reporter, the group held a prayer meeting. "All the wives or sweethearts whose husbands didn't come back seemed to know it. The others weren't worried. The Lord showed me what would happen."

Then she abruptly walked away, smiling.

Meanwhile, it fell to the Forest Service to notify Maude Powers of the death of her husband Robert, whose body was one of the first identified. He had been carrying a metal Standard Oil Company charge plate (these were the days before plastic bank cards), and he'd worn a bronze Forest Service badge and a metal Oklahoma A&M belt buckle, all of which survived the flames. (Vote's nickel-plated fire badge did not survive.)

Shortly after daylight Thomas approached Werner and asked if he was friendly with the Powers family. Werner said he didn't know them well because they were new to the district, but he agreed to accompany Thomas to carry the news to Maude Powers. She was making sandwiches and coffee for the fire crew when the two men arrived. When she heard that Robert was dead, she started to collapse. Werner caught her and she quickly recovered, ready to discuss with him whether to tell the children – Robert, nine, and Susan, seven – right away. They decided it would be better to do it before the children heard it from someone else. Bob and Sue took the news solemnly. Werner remained with the family until relatives showed up.

Within a few months, Mrs. Powers and the children moved back to her family home in Oklahoma City, but she and Werner kept in touch by letter. Eventually he made a trip to Oklahoma to see her. One thing led to another, and they married in January 1954.

"It was the best thing that ever happened to me," Werner said decades later. The family tried living in Willows, but the place had too many ghosts. Werner talked it over with his supervisor, Thomas, who well understood the problem and arranged a transfer for him some three hundred miles away, to the Sequoia National Forest in southern California. Red and Maude Werner were together for forty-five years, until her death in June of 1999.

Looking eastward downcanyon from a spot near the High Point.
NOTE FROM KARI GREER: The fireline at the bottom of this photo was both dozer
and handline; where it gets a little steeper is where the handline picks up. The
dozers were problematic; one was slipping a track, so the other had to do double
duty and put in line up toward High Point (south, at right) and then on top of
Powderhouse Ridge (north, at left, where Lafferty ran up). Vote, Werner, and
Casaurang each took resources from Powderhouse Turn to construct line
(Casaurang on Alder Springs Road with pumper trucks was more holding and spot
chasing), so Werner and his gang humped up to High Point; Vote and crew were
lining on the top of Rattlesnake Ridge, chasing the slopover.

Young Bob Powers followed in his father's footsteps.
He joined the Forest Service in 1962 as a firefighter in
California, served as assistant foreman on the Oak Grove
Hotshots, and went on to other fire and dispatch posts.

On one occasion, a close call on a fire brought back a
rush of memories of the Rattlesnake Fire. Bob Powers
was leading a crew of twenty when a fire roared out of a
canyon, breached firelines and roads, reduced twenty-
foot-high brush to charred stubble in seconds, and

headed straight for his crew. Powers shouted for everyone to run for it.

"I thought, *It's going to happen to me like it did to my dad*," Powers remembered. But they made it to a cleared safety zone and watched as the flames passed by.

AS FULL MORNING ARRIVED ON JULY 10, the lines were holding on what was left of the Rattlesnake Fire, but there were issues to sort out. Thomas decided to relieve Lafferty, who had worked through the night and was physically exhausted as well as emotionally drained. By the time Lafferty arrived home, after a lengthy detour to Fouts Springs for a difficult meeting with families of the victims, he was merely a ghost of himself.

"He was a kind man, everybody's friend," his wife Flora (or Mimi, as she was known) told me in a 2004 interview a few weeks before her death in Willows at the age of 92. "He tried to get the fire out of his mind, but I don't think he ever did. He went through all those emotions and then one day he said, 'Let's not talk about it anymore,' and he just didn't talk about it," his wife remembered.

Upon reading this remembrance in an earlier edition of this story, his fifth-born grandchild, Maureen C. Lafferty, wrote me about her memories of "Pappy," as the family called him. "I always wondered why he was so filled with anger and darkness inside of himself as I was growing up," Maureen said. On Fourth of July holidays, she told me, "Pappy" wouldn't allow his family to play with fireworks, not even sparklers. When Flora explained to the children that he had "a terrible sad memory of a very big fire he once experienced," Maureen figured it was "best to let it be," and to just think of the good times with her grandfather. Maureen said she loved him despite his negativity; he lived to the age of 93.

Lafferty did fight fire again, but he had become overcautious and unable to take necessary risks. He was transferred to a dispatch job at Willows, replacing Ripley, who had handled the Rattlesnake Fire radio traffic quickly and efficiently and was given a good post elsewhere. The rumor persisted that Lafferty "got religion" after the fire, but Flora Lafferty said Charlie had always had a religious side. Because they had lived mostly in isolated, rural places, it had been difficult to attend services, but they became regular churchgoers after Charlie transferred to Willows.

Upon retirement, Lafferty described the highlights of his long, eventful career in an oral history compiled for the Forest Service. He never once mentioned the Rattlesnake Fire.

"THAT WAS MY CAR."

HENRY ERHART WAS HAVING BREAKFAST at home in Dunsmuir, California, about 130 miles north of Willows, when his phone rang with an urgent call. Erhart was an arson detective for Region Five of the Forest Service, which covers eighteen national forests and a national grassland sited mostly within California, plus Hawaii and Guam and the Trust Territories of the Pacific Islands. A handful of Forest Service arson specialists are situated around the country, but California has its own squad, set up to handle the state's perennial troubles with incendiaries. The arson unit, established in 1918, was modeled on the Royal Canadian Mounted Police. Within a few years of its inception the detectives had cut losses from arson by 80 percent. By the time of the Rattlesnake Fire, though, their success had also reduced the number of detectives down from squad-like proportions; Erhart, fifty-six, was one of only three left in California.

Summoned early to the Rattlesnake Fire, Erhart arrived at the fire camp about 2 p.m. on July 10 with little doubt that he was on a manhunt. Almost nothing could explain the ignition except arson. Not only had there been no lightning or campfires nearby, but there were also no railroads or powerlines for miles around. A carelessly tossed cigarette or match can start a fire in matted duff or crushed grass, if conditions are just right, but those very fine fuels were not present here.

The sheriff and Gaither P. "Doc" Harper, a firefighter who had spent the night playing amateur sleuth – to surprisingly good effect – greeted Erhart on arrival. Harper, a lowly "fire-prevention aide" but no fool, had had his suspicions aroused while chatting with Silva, who'd told him about sighting the green Buick at Long Point Lookout minutes after the fire began. Harper sniffed around for more clues and learned about the sighting of the Buick by William Brown, the firefighter who had seen the vehicle in the bottom of Grindstone Canyon as he was driving away from the Chrome Fire. Harper passed along his gleanings to Erhart and pointed out Silva and his helper Pesonen in the chow line, where they were being waited on by, of all people, Stanford Philip Pattan.

"We were going through the chow line being served steak or scrambled eggs or something," Pesonen recalled. "A Forest Service investigator came up to me and said, 'I understand you may have written down something about a car.' I still had the note in my pocket with a description of the car and a number or two of the license plate."

Pattan overheard the conversation and became visibly agitated. In Pesonen's telling, when Erhart took him and Silva out of the chow line to question them in private, Pattan followed and volunteered the information that the Buick they were talking about was his.

"I think this fellow is describing my car," Pattan said. "I was up here yesterday squirrel hunting."

Erhart and Sheriff Sale later told a slightly different version of the incident in which Silva, the senior man, played the lead role and there was no mention of his underling Pesonen or his crumpled note: rank does have its prerogatives. The essentials, though, are the same: Pattan overheard the men talking about a green Buick, became visibly nervous, and volunteered the information that he'd driven a similar vehicle through the area the day before. Erhart, in a highly credible variation of Pesonen's account, quoted Pattan as saying, "That was my car; I'm Stanford Pattan – Phil Pattan's son."

Pattan offered them a hodgepodge of clumsy lies to explain his movements in the area the day before. He said he'd driven out from Willows and made a single loop up the Alder Springs Road. He'd stopped along the way, he said, to shoot his .22 rifle, had visited Long Point Lookout and the Alder Springs guard station, and had then driven home by a back road. Erhart thought Pattan appeared "very anxious to have us believe he was telling the truth" and he sent Pattan back to the chow line while he and Sheriff Sale talked things over.

Pattan, writhing in the first pangs of what would become agonized remorse, was overheard to say, "Damn it, they sent me to cook and what am I doing?"

It took Erhart and Sale less than five minutes to conclude that they very likely had their man, but as yet no proof. They then asked Pattan to take them along the route he claimed he'd driven the day before, and he agreed, and the tour became black comedy. Every time he said he was somewhere that might support his claim of innocence, there was no evidence to back him up. Every time he acknowledged that he had been in a place implying guilt, the evidence of his presence was plain.

"I tell you I had nothing to do with starting that fire," Pattan declared. He told the investigators he had never been in the bottom of Grindstone Canyon, where the witness Brown saw the green Buick. The law enforcement team found a freshly shot up picnic table and coffee can there, with holes from .22 bullets.

Pattan showed them a place along Alder Springs Road, above Powderhouse Turn and far from the scene of the fire, where he said he had fired his rifle. But no spent shell casings could be found there. He admitted, though, that he had fired some shots from Oleta Point, a few yards from the origin of the fire. Harper, the amateur detective who had attached himself to the investigation team, discovered five .22 shell casings at Oleta Point. Pattan acknowledged that they could be his. Remarkably, Erhart and Sale treated Harper like a full-fledged member of the investigation team, and he dogged their footsteps for days. They allowed Harper to interview witnesses, take notes, and have a turn or two questioning Pattan. Erhart made a favorable reference to Harper in his written report, citing his handwritten notes as a source to make a point. The cooperative spirit on the team was noteworthy and contributed to the speed of the investigation, though probably not the outcome: Pattan was a marked man from the start.

The investigators returned Pattan to the fire camp and left him under the eye of a deputy while they went to further check his story. Pattan had claimed that he'd learned about the fire from Mrs. Powers and Mrs. Silva when he'd stopped at the Alder Springs guard station. When interviewed, the women said to the contrary that Pattan had known about the fire when he'd arrived.

Pattan said he had two beers at the Elkhorn Tavern around noon. But the bartender told the lawmen about his glance at the clock at 2 p.m. when Pattan came into the place. Pattan left shortly thereafter, the bartender said – just in time to start the fire.

The investigation team returned to the fire camp, ate dinner, and then took Pattan back to the Glenn County jail in Willows. By all reports, including Pattan's, he was not roughed up

> Pattan was a marked man from the start.

physically. The questioning, though, continued on through a sleepless night. The lawmen told Pattan about the eyewitness testimony contradicting his story and flatly accused him of setting the Chrome and Rattlesnake fires. By 4 a.m., Pattan had begun to hedge.

He admitted for the first time that he had stopped at the Tankersley house and had seen the Chrome Fire from there, not from the town of Elk Creek as he had claimed earlier. And yes, he had told Mrs. Powers and Mrs. Silva he had seen smoke; he had lied when he'd told them he'd learned about the fire from the two women. Again, yes, he had been in the bottom of Grindstone Canyon plinking with his .22 – but he insisted that he had not set either fire. He'd told those lies, he said, to explain away the reports about a green Buick, which made things look dark for him.

The interview concluded at 5:30 a.m. on July 11, according to the transcript, which by coincidence was about ten minutes after the Rattlesnake Fire was declared under control. The fire had briefly come back to life at about 7 p.m. the previous evening, July 10, when a downslope wind started up, repeating the fatal wind behavior of the previous night. The wind on the evening of July 10 was not as strong, but it pushed flames across the southern edge of the fireline and burned an additional 80 acres. All told, the Rattlesnake Fire lasted a little more than a day and a half, burned 1,200 to 1,300 acres, and was fought by 333 to 525 men (accounts of acreage and manpower vary). The cost to suppress it came to $50,000 – and the lives of fifteen men.

At daybreak on July 11 the investigation team, Harper still included, took Pattan to breakfast. It must have been a bleary, tense gathering. Pattan's story was breaking down, but there was no physical evidence to tie him to the fire. The lawmen thought they had the right man, but as yet their case would not stand up in court and they knew it. They needed something more, a confession or physical evidence tying Pattan to the fire.

Sheriff Sale talking with Stan Pattan about his Buick.

They all drove back to Oleta Point, where Erhart ramped up the pressure.

"Here, I'll show you how you did it," Erhart told Pattan. He flipped a lighted match out of the car window into the gray ash of what had been thick brush just a few days before.

"You didn't even get out of your car, did you, Stan?"

Pattan again denied his guilt.

The investigation team had other people to interview, so they sent Pattan back to Willows, where he caught a couple of hours' sleep in the sheriff's office. Erhart returned to town by late afternoon and held a strategy conference with District Attorney Larimer. They decided to try to break Pattan's story with a polygraph machine, and Pattan "readily agreed" to the test, according to Erhart. Harry Cooper, a state agent who specialized in lie-detector examinations, was summoned and arrived in Willows by nightfall.

The investigators, meanwhile, obtained from the *Willows Journal* a set of photographs of the bodies on the hillside. They spread the brutal images on the table in front of Pattan. Fifty years later, Pattan recalled that jarring moment as though it had happened the day before. "Yes, they showed me the pictures," he said without hesitation, one of his few clear memories of those days.

The most imposing image they showed him is not immediately recognizable as a group of bodies; the photo looks more like a pile of blackened logs with branches sticking out every which way. Even when the forms are recognized as bodies, it is still difficult to make an accurate count, because they are in such disorder. In other shots taken from a distance, the bodies seem lost in a grayed-out landscape that stretches out hundreds of barren yards in every direction. The firefighters in this group had no chance of escape.

"Why? Why did you do it?" Erhart pressed Pattan. The missionaries were not the only ones asking the question why.

Pattan, haggard from lack of sleep and emotional distress, smoked cigarette after cigarette. But he said nothing to incriminate himself. Cooper, the lie-detector technician, sat him down next to the box-like machine and attached tubes and wires to Pattan's chest, arms, and fingers; the monitors checked his respiratory rate, the sweatiness of his fingers, and his pulse and blood pressure. Today's polygraph machine is more technically sophisticated, but it monitors the same bodily reactions to stress.

It was like a scene from an old detective movie. Every time Pattan was asked if he'd set the fires, the needles skittered across the scroll paper. "The reaction of the lie detector thoroughly indicated that Pattan had been telling untruths and that he did set the fire," Erhart wrote in his report.

None of this was admissible in court. In 1953, the courts operated under a landmark ruling by the U.S. Court of Appeals in the District of Columbia that scientific evidence to be admitted must first be accepted by the scientific community. In 1923, in *Frye v. United States*, a murder case, the court of appeals had ruled that results from a unigraph (a precursor of the polygraph) could not be admitted as evidence because the scientific community did not agree that it gave reliable results.

The legal and scientific situation is little changed today; polygraph tests are inadmissible in a handful of states, but in other states they are sometimes admissible – under certain conditions and at the discretion of the judge. The scientific community is divided on the tests' accuracy, but virtually no one claims that a machine can always spot a lie.

Man Confesses To Setting Forest Fire Fatal To 15

WILLOWS, Calif. (AP) — Police are holding a jobless twenty-six-year-old man who they say has confessed starting a forest fire which took 15 lives Thursday—so he could get a job fighting it.

Glenn County Sheriff Lyle G. Sale picked up Stanfor P. Patton for questioning as he was working at his new job of cook at the fire control camp in Mendocino National Forest.

Patton was without money to support his pregnant wife and three children. He said he last worked as a crop duster, but that job "ran out" on him. Local authorities, who had known Patton since he came to Willows with his family 20 years ago, said he had never been in trouble.

Note "Patton" misspelling

AFTER A LITTLE OVER AN HOUR of questioning with the machine, Pattan sent word that he was ready to talk. "The pictures certainly helped break him," Sheriff Sale said afterward. "When he saw those, I believe he realized for the first time what he had done." But so did watching the skittering needles of the polygraph.

A sheriff's deputy using shorthand took down Pattan's first confession, beginning at 10:30 p.m. on July 11. Pattan went over the same ground, beginning the story over again a little later at 11:10 p.m., as a court reporter made a verbatim record. The investigators were taking no chances, because without Pattan's confession they had no case. Pattan had been seen driving through the mountains, but that is no crime, and no one could place him within a mile of either fire. If Pattan retracted his statements, he had a plausible defense even by 1953 legal standards. Sheriff Sale later told Pattan that he had

145

put himself in jail with his confession. Sale meant that as a compliment, and a half-century later Pattan still regarded it in that light. He seemed actually relieved to have gotten the thing off his chest.

Erhart, ever the bulldog, desperately wanted to lock up the case by establishing a physical link between Pattan and the fires – a case like this was not one he wanted to lose over some minor missed detail. The detective got some much-needed sleep on July 12 and went back to the mountains the next day to take photographs, measure distances, and do mop-up interviews with witnesses.

He also recruited a posse of sorts – three sheriff's deputies – to hunt for a piece of evidence he thought might have survived the fire: the single wooden match Pattan had flicked to start the fire. It seemed a fool's errand; the proverbial needle in a haystack should be easier to find than a burned match in the debris of a wildfire. But Erhart's posse looked first at the site of the Chrome Fire and, surprisingly, turned up not one but three burned matches. Granted, the Chrome Fire had not been nearly as intense and destructive as the Rattlesnake Fire, but the discovery of the matches there raised hopes.

Erhart went to the spot where Pattan said he had tossed the single match that started the Rattlesnake Fire – 240 feet up the Alder Springs Road from Oleta Point. Erhart staked out a rectangle ten feet by six feet and used white string to divide it into a checkerboard of roughly three-foot squares; arson detectives use the same gridding technique to this day, except the squares to be examined are smaller. In a later, more scientifically advanced age, an investigation team discovered a small arson device, hidden amid burned debris, composed of wooden matches held around a cigarette by a rubber band. It started the 2006 Esperanza Fire, which killed the five crewmen of USFS Engine 57. After a general survey of two acres of southern California ground, the investigation team had narrowed the search and began to construct a four-by-eight-foot grid with one-by-one squares marked off. A team member, standing nearby, looked down at the ground and saw a little teepee of burned matches and a cigarette butt. "What do you think of that?" he remarked. Using only the naked eye, he had spotted what turned out to be the arson device. Such small and seemingly impossible-to-find items have a long history in arson fires. Almost fifty years after the Rattlesnake Fire, a DNA sample from a chewed piece of hotdog left in a campfire put arson investigators on a search for those responsible for the 2001 Thirtymile Fire in Washington state. The fire killed four young firefighters. The investigators these many years later have not yet found a DNA match, and that case still remains open.

On the Rattlesnake Fire, the posse completed an initial search of the marked-off grid without finding anything. Erhart had the men switch squares and repeat the exercise, checking each other's work. Again, no results. This went on for two hours.

It was Deputy Sheriff Dan Ellis who finally announced "Here it is!" and held up the charred remains of a single wooden match.

IN 1953, BEFORE THE AGE OF DNA analysis, there was no way to link the match that started the Rattlesnake Fire to Pattan, and it would be difficult if not impossible today, considering that the match was burned. For example, the Esperanza Fire arson device had no identifiable DNA. Raymond Oyler's genetic evidence was found, however, on recovered devices at two fires that he set several months before the Esperanza Fire, on the ends of cigarettes he'd apparently puffed to get them burning. A jury decided those fires were part of a long series of fires set by Oyler with similar devices, culminating in the fatal Esperanza Fire. Finding the match at the origin of the Rattlesnake Fire did provide a physical link to the details of Pattan's confession, if not to his actual person. "This evidence was all carefully preserved and is now in possession of the District Attorney, Glenn County," Erhart wrote at the conclusion of his report. Like the Mounties, Erhart had his man, with help from the local law enforcement officers and Doc Harper.

In later years, District Attorney Larimer and Sheriff Sale would joke between themselves that Erhart and the sheriff had been given too much credit for the investigation, and that Larimer had played a vital but overlooked role. Clifford Larimer, the district attorney's son, in 2013 wrote an article about the fire and subsequently exchanged emails with me about it. "It was my dad who Pattan had actually confessed to," complained the younger Larimer, a longtime California newsman. "The omission didn't seem to bother my father. He and Lyle had long been friends. Lyle never came forward publicly to set the press and public straight, and over the years there was plenty of light banter involving the oversight when my dad, Lyle and their friends got together for drinks, barbecue, dinner or poolside talk."

The Larimers and Pattans lived next door to each other for a few years when Stanford Pattan was growing up, Clifford Larimer recalled, but he was not a close friend of Stanford, who was ten years older. "The next time I became aware of Stan was when Dad was talking to Mom years later and he was telling her he knew who 'had done it' and he thought he'd be able to get him to confess," the younger Larimer wrote.

Pattan was charged with second-degree murder, but a Glenn County grand jury decided that he had not intended to kill or even harm anyone, a necessary precondition for a murder indictment. The grand jury instead reduced the charges to two felony counts of willful burning, one for the Rattlesnake Fire and one for the smaller Chrome Fire set earlier in the day.

Pattan remembers looking out the window of his cell on an upper floor of the Glenn County Jail in Willows, during those first days after the fire. Newsmen swarmed below "like a lynch mob howling for my blood." The experience chilled any desire Pattan may have had to defend himself in public. During courtroom appearances, he restricted his comments for the record to "Guilty, sir" for each of the two counts of the indictment. Asked at sentencing a few days later if he wished to say anything on his own behalf, he stood mute.

Pattan was sentenced to San Quentin prison, but he was lucky in his experience there, as such things go. He was young and good-looking and could have fared very badly. He worked as a medical orderly, however, tending to prisoner ailments at night when no doctor was present, which allowed him to sleep in the hospital unit away from the general prison population. During the day he worked as a painter. "We had a lot of talented artists in the population," he says, "and they put us to work painting murals in the mess halls." Pattan developed his talent through an art correspondence course, the kind once advertised on the inside covers of matchbooks.

While he served his time, his father Philip moved away in shame from the town of Willows. Pattan probably would not have come back to Glenn County, he says, except in those days a prisoner had to have a job before he could qualify for parole. Friends offered him work on their farm, and after three years in prison, he was released on probation. His civil rights were restored under an amnesty program available at that time after successful completion of probation, which took him an additional three years. Clifford Larimer told me he'd heard that Pattan had a period of heavy drinking after his release, but by the time I knew him he lived a sober life.

One of Pattan's jobs soon after he left prison was driving a hospital ambulance, which led to yet another disastrous experience. After Sale lost an election as Glenn County Sheriff, he worked as a hospital administrator. Years after he had arrested Stan Pattan for the fire, Sale gave him the ambulance job to help him get back on his feet. Pattan was on duty one day when a call came in about a vehicle accident between Willows and Elk Creek, not far from the site of the Rattlesnake Fire. A speeding pickup truck had gone off the highway and struck a utility pole. Bill Flanagan, the California Highway Patrol trooper (and former Willows Town Constable) who handled the wreck, said the young male driver had been trying to beat a friend's time between Willows and Elk Creek when he lost control at a notorious spot called Mitchell's Curve. The boy was severely injured and his girl passenger was killed. When Pattan drove up to the wreck scene in the ambulance, Flanagan tried to stop him from going on to the pickup: Flanagan had identified the dead girl as Pattan's sixteen-year-old daughter Susan, one of his and Portia Lee's four children. But Pattan told Flanagan that he and Susan had not been close, and he needed to do his job.

(Bill Flanagan, who told me this story in 2014 when he was 88, said he and Pattan had lived next door to each other for a time when they were young and had been casual friends.)[4]

---

[4] William "Bill" Flanagan died at home in Willows on June 30, 2016, at the age of 90. He and his family moved from Moscow, Idaho, to Willows when he was five years old. Bill served as Town Constable for six years; he joined the California Highway Patrol in 1955, retiring after 26 years, as a sergeant in the Willows office. He was married to his wife, Nettie Lou, for 65 years. They had two sons, Michael and Robert, five grandchildren, and five great-grandchildren.

A VIRTUAL RIVER OF AIR

S THE ARSON INVESTIGATION PROCEEDED in the immediate aftermath of the fire, fire weather meteorologists conducted a separate inquiry into the causes of the fatal downhill wind shift. Two researchers from the Pacific Southwest Forest and Range Experiment Station of the Forest Service traveled to the site the day after the fire. For two nights in a row, July 10 and 11, they took dozens of wind readings along Rattlesnake Ridge, Alder Springs Road, Powderhouse Turn, and the side road leading to the dynamite shed.

On both nights, winds shifted in the evening exactly as it had on July 9, from upslope to downslope. The winds weren't terribly strong – the highest recorded was twenty miles an hour. But the winds were from the right direction, over the lip of the ridge and down the canyon.

Though no observations were taken the night of the fatalities, witnesses estimated the wind at the top at far stronger than twenty miles an hour. Normal nighttime downslope winds are light, from two to five miles an hour, and thus don't explain the magnitude of what happened. Perhaps two wind events occurred, a normal evening downslope breeze followed by something much more powerful? If so, that would match the fire's abruptly changing behavior, from the initial run up the side of Powderhouse Ridge, which nearly caught Lafferty and the others heading up the ridge, to the ninety-degree shift and the fire's subsequent powerful run down Powderhouse Canyon, the run that caught fifteen men.

Looking back up toward the Missionary Spot Fire (center of photo) from the firefighters' escape route. Powderhouse Turn is at top right, with the very top (lip) of the canyon far up to the left beyond the photo's edge.

The official Rattlesnake Fire report, using data collected by these meteorologists, discounts a two-event theory. Their report describes the wind on the Rattlesnake Fire as part of a normal pattern for the terrain and time of day. Because hot air rises, daytime heating caused the fire to move uphill. At about 9 p.m. the winds subsided "because the sun had dropped behind the ridges to the west and surface heating had thus stopped." The lull that occurred at about 9:45 p.m. came about "as a result of a give and take process between the last passage of upslope thermal currents and the first downward movement of heavier, cool, evening air."

The downslope wind took over at 10 p.m. because cool air descends. "This downslope movement of air is a normal evening occurrence caused by cooler, denser air seeking a lower elevation," the report concluded. "As a result of this general change in wind direction and the increased wind velocity inherent in the initial stages of this situation, the behavior of the entire fire was affected."

In other words, nothing special had occurred or needed to be learned about wind and fire behavior from the Rattlesnake Fire.

A few months later, however, W.R. Krumm, a fire-weather meteorologist based in Missoula, Montana, analyzed the wind data and came to an opposite conclusion: an exceptional two-event wind scenario was *necessary* to explain the fire's behavior.

Normal night cooling does not cause winds strong enough to account for what happened on the Rattlesnake Fire, Krumm contended. The cooling effect

155

at night occurs close to the earth's skin, where temperature change is most pronounced. Thus, air drains to lower elevations and canyon bottoms, gathering speed along the way. This means that the downslope wind effect is strongest in the *bottoms* of canyons, which is counterintuitive considering the bottoms appear protected from wind. As a consequence, fires tend to "creep" downslope at night, not explode down the slope.

On the Rattlesnake Fire, though, the wind blew most fiercely along the *tops* of ridges, such as Powderhouse Turn. Witnesses attested to this on the night of July 9, and the careful weather observations on July 10 and 11 showed the same thing, confirming the witness accounts: the highest wind velocities occurred on the ridge tops, not down in the canyon bottoms. And the fire did anything but creep.

"To the author this would suggest that the air mass changed when the fire commenced to burn fiercely shortly after 10 p.m.," Krumm wrote in his February 1954 analysis.

The wind, though, had to be strong enough to turn the fire ninety degrees and send it hurtling down into the canyon. The flames chasing Lafferty and the others up the side of the slope should have caught them and burned to the top of Powderhouse Ridge, a scant hundred yards away, in just seconds if all the fire had to overcome was a normal evening downslope light wind. It took more than half an hour for the flames to burn against the wind for the last hundred yards up to Powderhouse Ridge – at 11 p.m. With just a normal evening breeze, the fire also should have spared and not chased the fifteen others who were headed down the canyon. A powerful contrary force was required to turn that fire to plunging down the canyon.

For the fire report to be correct Grindstone Canyon would have to be filled with air collected from the normal evening cooling; no lesser volume of air could have produced such a potent wind at the top of Powderhouse Canyon. But Krumm considered the report's explanation for the air mass illogical; the volume of cool air required was staggering, far too much to be gathered simply from the normal cooling process allowed for in the fire report. Something else had to explain it – explain why the wind had been so fierce, so powerful. The answer had to fill Grindstone Canyon to overflowing with rapidly moving air.

And Krumm found it.

On the afternoon of July 9, an inland trough of low pressure extending from California into Oregon and southern Idaho began to deepen. At the same time, hundreds of miles to the west, a high-pressure ridge was building over the Pacific Ocean, on a line parallel to the coasts of California, Oregon, Washington, and British Columbia. By 7 p.m., the wind-shift line – the edge between the two pressure areas – had moved east over northern California. Winds above Sacramento, Oakland, and other cities were measured at about five thousand feet, blowing hard from the west and northwest. At the same time, winds closer to the ground were relatively calm across the area.

The wind-shift line pressed eastward from the coast, running into the Coast Range just to the west of the Rattlesnake Fire. The winds built up behind the Coast Range and sought escape through gaps in the mountains and passes at the tops of ridges. When the winds poured through the gaps, their velocity was increased by the *Venturi effect* – gases and liquids increase speed when constricted, just as a river develops rapids in narrow chutes. One of the gaps was Mendocino Pass, a jagged opening that marks the head of Grindstone Canyon, about 30 miles west of the fire. Mendocino Pass is about five thousand feet above sea level, an elevation where the west winds blew hard that day.

A virtual river of fast-moving air poured down through Mendocino Pass and filled Grindstone Canyon west of the fire to the brim. This phenomenon was happening up and down the Coast Range: strong winds reported on July 9 nearly capsized small boats on Stony Gorge Reservoir, south of the Rattlesnake Fire, after passing through a low gap south of Mendocino Pass.

Nothing in Grindstone Canyon slowed the wind. Within minutes of 10:15 p.m. on July 9, the great ocean of wind pouring down Grindstone Canyon spilled over the lip of Powderhouse Turn, driving the fire down Powderhouse Canyon. The normal evening cooling effect already had occurred and had stoked the fire that chased Lafferty and the nine missionaries. The mass of air now borne on the new wind was so huge that it continued, though with lesser force, for the next two days, which is what the fire weather meteorologists measured.

At least that was Krumm's theory, which happened to run counter to the official fire report's explanation of normal evening cooling. Krumm offered his conclusion with some hesitation. "The author believes that this is possible, but the evidence is not strong enough to say positively," he wrote.

The wind that turned the Rattlesnake Fire down the canyon resulted from a "mild subsidence," the sudden dropping of an air mass at great speed, Krumm concluded; a major subsidence, on the other hand, can cause hurricane-strength winds of seventy to ninety miles an hour, far stronger than what witnesses reported on the Rattlesnake Fire. The phenomenon of subsidence was well known at the time: dramatic downslope winds are called Santa Ana winds in southern California, Diablo winds in the San Francisco Bay area, Chinook winds when they sweep down the Front Range of the Rocky Mountains, and East winds when they blow in western Washington and Oregon. All of these occur frequently.

No one, though, expected a major downslope wind after dark in this part of northern California. The fire supervisors – Thomas, Ewing, and Lafferty – had much experience with Santa Ana winds in southern California. None of them had translated that experience into preparation for a similar event on the Rattlesnake Fire.

Thomas came closest among the three to addressing the issue afterward.

"We always anticipate and plan on a shift in the wind," he told the Glenn County grand jury. "It's usually a gentle shift. It usually shifts from an up-canyon to a down-canyon at night. We contemplate and plan on it." He offered no explanation of why the wind shift on the Rattlesnake Fire was so sudden and powerful and not the "gentle shift" he described.

Krumm's theory has stood up over the years. The first fire-behavior course for firefighters was not developed until 1959, six years after the fire. Today, the Rattlesnake Fire has become an object lesson for California firefighters and others, proof that fires can burn fiercely downslope at night in unexpected places. "Fire behavior was the largest factor in this accident," states a recent teaching manual for Cal Fire firefighters.

The exact cause of strong downslope winds, often called sundowners because they occur in late afternoon or evening, is not fully understood, but it involves cooling and heating at ground level combined with a tug-of-war between high- and low-pressure areas in the atmosphere. The ground level cooling may pull down the upper-level winds under certain conditions, bringing on sundowners.

The effect can be truly astonishing – and deadly dangerous. The most phenomenal California sundowner in recorded history occurred June 17, 1859. The event was monitored and reported on by an engineering boat from what then was called the U.S. Coast Survey (now known as the U.S. National Geodetic Survey).

The survey boat, anchored near Santa Barbara, which is famous for its sundowners, basked in beautiful California June weather with temperatures in the mid-80s – until about 1 p.m. when a northwest wind started up. At 2 p.m. the boat's crew recorded an astounding temperature of 133 degrees amid a dust storm that turned daylight to a dusky twilight.

"No human being could withstand such heat," the survey report declared. Animals dropped dead where they stood, fruits and vegetables shriveled and died, birds died in flight and fell to the earth. By 8 p.m. the horror was gone and the temperature had dropped to 77 degrees.

FOR FIREFIGHTERS, IT IS ENOUGH TO KNOW that they must be prepared for such events. For the fifteen men who died on the Rattlesnake Fire, it means their loss very likely has saved lives and will continue to do so. Considering the spirit of the missionaries, who were willing to risk extreme privation and even death to convert pagan tribes, and who believed the motto "To Die Is to Gain," they may well have gone to their fiery deaths without remorse if they had known that their sacrifice would save the lives of many others for decades to come. They were not a selfish bunch.

"THIS GENTLEMAN HAS COMMITTED A GRAVE CRIME."

THE FIRE AND ITS AFTERMATH caused days of sensational headlines in northern California; the story had bounce, as they say in the news business. Reports of massive loss of life and "pretty rugged" photos (according to a Forest Service summary), were followed by rumors of arson and then by the confession of the arsonist, the son of a well-regarded Forest Service engineer. Curiously, the fire did not cause banner headlines nationwide, as usually happens with multiple fatalities in the line of duty, and the reason lies partly in the timing. The firefighters were killed late on a Friday, and news of the deaths was even later in coming. Late Friday is a traditional black hole for news, a time often used for announcements of bad news made by politicians and others who want to see a story fade away from lack of attention as the weekend begins and newspaper attention turns to the big Sunday editions. The timing of the Rattlesnake Fire story fit the black hole scenario perfectly.

The story ran as a single column tucked to the side of page 3 of the Saturday *Los Angeles Times*, which should have been expected to give it a screaming headline on the front page. The news arrived even later in time zones to the east. By then the Saturday run of papers had ended entirely, the Sunday papers were mostly ready, and weary editors were headed for home; the story appeared for the first time in the *New York Times* on page 28 of its Sunday edition, with a stale Friday dateline, as though it were a second-day story.

The religious twist also made the story an oddity, if not a kind of pariah, for news organizations. Most accounts identified the dead not as fifteen firefighters, which they certainly were, but as fourteen missionaries and a Forest Service ranger. Four years earlier in 1949, the Mann Gulch Fire had commanded headlines across the nation when twelve smokejumpers and a wilderness guard (a former smokejumper) were killed, the first-ever deaths by fire for the elite airborne men of the firefighting world. Not until the South Canyon Fire four and a half decades later would flames again claim the lives of smokejumpers. The Rattlesnake Fire, even with two more deaths than the Mann Gulch Fire, was relegated to a column in the religious section of *Time* magazine. *Life* magazine, which had run a multi-page spread of photos of Mann Gulch, ran a news roundup in its next edition after the Rattlesnake Fire, including California fire stories, but improbably said not a thing about the Rattlesnake Fire.

The arson angle, however, did draw considerable attention from less prominent publications. *American Forests* magazine carried a story about the fire by the lucky reporter who was there, Gleeson, in which he recounted his personal experience. *Official Detective Stories*, a pulp magazine, contained a lurid account in its September 1953 issue that, miraculously, included thoughts and quotations from Ranger Powers, who presumably spoke to them from beyond the grave. More than a year later, the *Saturday Evening Post* published a more credible account of Erhart's successful arson investigation as a highlight in a story about California arson detectives.

Less than a month after the fire, a radio show called *Bill Guyman Covers California* reported a "new angle" – a source had told Guyman that a crew of loggers had refused to go into Powderhouse Canyon before the mission crew was sent there because the location was "highly dangerous." He asked his radio listeners why the mission crew had been sent down to fight the "dangerous" fire after such a refusal. "This may just be the surface of something that has been covered up," Guyman suggested.

A subsequent Forest Service inquiry confirmed the refusal but concluded that the hazards of steep terrain – and not the dangers of the Missionary Spot Fire – were the reason the loggers had refused to go into the canyon. The mission crew had been sent to the spot fire long *before* the loggers' refusal, the inquiry found; the mission boys were sent when it was thought to be a safe enough assignment. Virtually every big fatal wildfire spurs a round of conspiracy theories, many far more accusatory than Guyman's unsubstantiated radio remarks.

One lurid theory current to this day, for example, concerns the 1949 Mann Gulch Fire that killed the thirteen firefighters. In order to explain how the fire got below the firefighters unobserved, a few former smokejumpers hold to the theory that the Forest Service ranger in charge of the fire, John Robert Jansson, started or accelerated the fire himself. In fact, Jansson was nearly killed by the fire that eyewitnesses testified was burning out of control when he first approached it.

Blaming an evil outside agent for horrible events happens with predictable regularity, and fatal wildfires are no exception. It's said that the South Canyon Fire was started or accelerated by the elderly lover of one of the women firefighters who was killed; he supposedly flew a private plane to a secret landing field nearby, set the fire, and departed the same way. That fire actually was started by an observed lightning strike. When an arsonist starts a fire, however, as happened with the Rattlesnake and Esperanza fires, there is a ready target for blame by survivors who need one.

BY THE TIME THE GLENN COUNTY GRAND JURY heard testimony in the Rattlesnake Fire arson case, on July 30, just three weeks after the event, passions had begun to cool. Pattan had made a full confession, which brought a sense of relief. "Pattan's confession threw the situation into reverse to some degree," a Forest Service public information specialist reported. After the confession, "the general temper of the community indicates a desire for everyone to get away from the subject as soon as convenient." The Forest Service also issued a statement citing Pattan's previous employment as a fire guard and emergency firefighter and his father's "long-time and faithful" record with the agency. Nonetheless, Pattan stood accused of the murder of two of the fifteen victims, the two for whom there was the clearest evidence of identity: Powers, who had been recognized by his badge, metal credit card, and

Oklahoma Aggies belt buckle; and Sherman, who had left behind a young widow, Gerry, and not much else – a remnant of gray trousers, a scrap of a blue and white striped shirt, a bronze cowboy belt buckle ... and a watch.

"Would you describe that wristwatch and band that you found?" asked Charles Frost, assistant district attorney, of Howard Sweet, the deputy coroner.

"The wristwatch on this body was burned so badly that the watch – you couldn't tell the make, but there was a metal elastic band with the initials R and S in large letters."

Raymond Sherman was the only victim with the initials R.S., and the identification of his body from the watchband ended any legal interest in his belongings. The watch's glass lens had melted in the heat and had picked up tiny bits of shale, making it unreadable. Sherman's things were tucked into an envelope and, when no one claimed them, stored at Forest Service headquarters in Willows. The watch remained there and kept its secrets for half a century.

The swing in popular sentiment began to undermine the case for murder charges. On top of that, word had leaked out about Pattan's many personal misfortunes. "This is the story of Stanford Pattan," Gleeson began a front-page article in the *Willows Journal* a few days after the fire. (Gleeson's byline identified him as "regional editor," a promotion that apparently followed his big scoop by just hours.)

Gleeson portrayed Pattan as a likeable but irresponsible mope who had never been in real trouble in his life. Phrases such as "navy veteran" and "highly respected family" were sprinkled throughout the text. No questions were raised about his possible innocence or insanity. Pattan was mentally competent when he lit the fire, and he admitted that he had done it. But Gleeson detailed the domestic troubles and severe headaches that had bedeviled Pattan, creating a portrait of a mildly sympathetic figure and not a vicious criminal. "Headaches or heartaches, Stanford Philip Pattan, who today sits brooding in his cell at the county jail, must be having his share of both," Gleeson concluded.

For once, justice was swift, but the swing in sympathy for Pattan could go only so far. After the grand jury refused to indict Pattan on the murder charges and instead returned two felony counts of willful burning, the court on August 3 accepted Pattan's guilty pleas to both counts, less than a month after the fire. When Pattan was sentenced four days later, however, Judge W.T. Belieu was tougher than expected. He first denied a defense request for probation and then passed the sentence of one to ten years on each count, to be served consecutively, so Pattan faced up to twenty years in prison. A serious crime had been committed, the judge said, for which there was no excuse. "This gentleman has committed a grave crime against society and one to which society is entitled to protection. Punishment is not to be made lightly, or little, so that society ceases to have any protection."

Pattan fell into a deep depression. His guards at the jail reported that they were having him paint signs and other things to shake him out of it. He seemed to like painting and had a flair for it.

Pattan also tried out religion: he mentioned to a newspaper reporter during one of his brief court appearances the startling news that he was considering joining New Tribes Mission when he got out of prison. This came as a revelation to the mission directors. "For the first time, I have really read the Bible – both the Old and the New Testament," Pattan told the *Chico Enterprise-Record*'s Lee Soto, who was following the story after his timely visit to the Fouts Springs camp before the fire. "I am a baptized Baptist, and before this happened I guess I was about average in religion. If I can, when this is over, I want to do missionary work. Maybe with the New Tribes Mission, or maybe I can rejoin the navy and study for the ministry."

Pattan's remarks threw New Tribes Mission a moral curveball. The mission members had been careful to say in public speech that they were praying for Pattan and bore him no ill will. "We hold no grudge against any man," said Hare, the camp director. The Forest Service gave the missionaries much credit for helping to calm animosity and community anger. "The attitudes of the New Tribes Mission members were extremely helpful in keeping rash statements and attacks on the Forest Service to a minimum," the agency's information specialist reported. Accepting Pattan as a missionary trainee, however, might take forgiveness to a breaking point. "The Lord might speak to his heart," Joe Knutsen, a mission official, told Soto. "But he will have to get himself squared away before we will take him."

Pattan's jailhouse conversion did not last as long as his time in prison, but it did have an effect. Representatives of the mission, including Etherton, the dentist who had barely survived the fire, visited him at San Quentin. The missionaries and Pattan remembered that meeting in very different ways.

"He came to know the Lord as his Savior through their faithful witness," Johnston recorded in his history.

Pattan remembered feeling relief when the missionaries said they bore him no ill will, and the memory helped him stay out of trouble after that. He believed in God, he said, but he was no churchgoer.

"THEY DID NOT DIE IN VAIN."

THE RATTLESNAKE FIRE WAS YET ANOTHER body blow to the Forest Service, for by the middle of the 20th century the agency's war on fire was running up a heavy casualty list. Between the years 1936, the first year after the agency instituted the 10 a.m. policy of suppressing all fires by the morning after their discovery, and 1957, when the Forest Service convened a historic task force on firefighter safety, there were sixteen fires on National Forests in which seventy-nine men were burned to death. Eight of those fires killed more than one man. The 1957 report was submitted to the Chief of the Forest Service by a task force including W.R. "Bud" Moore, V.A. Parker, C.M. Countryman, L.K. Mays, and A.W. Greeley. They reviewed six of the fires intensively, including the Rattlesnake Fire, and proposed what to this day remains the bedrock document of firefighter safety, the Ten Standard Firefighting Orders.

Though no lines were drawn from a specific fire to a specific order, two of the orders could have come straight from the Rattlesnake Fire: post lookouts when there is possible danger, and keep informed on fire weather conditions and forecasts.

The immediate effect of the fire, however, was limited to a formal investigation and report. The chief of the Forest Service in 1953, Richard E. McArdle, charged a board of review to look into all aspects of the Rattlesnake Fire, including possible negligence. "We can't restore these men to the widows and orphans from whom they have been snatched away," McArdle wrote. "But if ever an obligation was clear this one is – to see to the extent that it is within our power to do so, that it never happens again."

God along with the supervisors was to stand in the dock, according to McArdle's instructions. "If it was caused by the negligence of any one in the Forest Service, we want to know it," McArdle continued. "If it was an act of God, and by any chance beyond our control, we want to know that."

The Rattlesnake board of review was made up entirely of senior Forest Service officials: Edward P. Cliff, assistant chief; Jay H. Price, regional forester; C. Otto Lindh, regional forester; Lawrence K. Mays, assistant regional forester; and H. Dean Cochran, chief of personnel. There were no outside experts, nor even personnel from other fire agencies – not even from other federal agencies in California or the state fire ranks.

The situation today has evolved and oversight has broadened. But fire agencies struggle to produce credible reports in the very short times often allotted them. Some argue that severe events happen only infrequently and do not justify the heavy costs of a standing body of professional investigators, and they have a point – the interval between double-digit multiple fatalities for wildland firefighters at the time of this writing was almost two decades, far longer than in the 1935 to 1957 interval. The long time gap between the South Canyon

Fire of 1994 and the Yarnell Hill Fire of 2013 surely came in part because of the near-tsunami of safety improvements following the South Canyon event.

In the last several decades, the investigation process has gradually and not always successfully moved away from an emphasis on identifying mistakes and assigning responsibility toward understanding the motives and circumstances behind complex events – and learning from them.

In the wake of a troubled South Canyon Fire investigation, however, one wildfire fatality investigation after another has been criticized, rightly or wrongly, for a lack of professionalism, short deadlines, and the willful disregard of mistakes by senior management. The atmosphere and attitudes surrounding fire investigations have grown even more contentious as a result of lawsuits by families of victims and federal legislation that in effect criminalizes wildland fire management decisions when negligence is found or alleged. These complex issues are compounded even further by instant and often unrestrained criticism and second-guessing now common on and exacerbated by social media.

In the case of the South Canyon Fire, two senior Forest Service investigators refused to sign the official investigation report, though one later relented when edits were negotiated. Seven years later, survivors of the 2001 Thirtymile Fire, which took the lives of four wildland firefighters, challenged and won revision of questionable findings made by investigators on that fire, findings that blamed the firefighters for ignoring an order that may have saved their lives. Pressed by legislators from the state of Washington, where the fire took place, Congress passed a bill requiring review of all Forest Service fireline deaths by the Office of Inspector General of the U.S. Department of Agriculture, the Forest Service's parent agency. Other subsequent OIG investigations, initially clumsy on account of a lack of experience – but significantly better as time went on – have raised the prospect of criminal charges for fire managers when something goes wrong on the job. As a direct result of the threat of legal action on so many fronts, many firefighters or fire managers have refused to give testimony about fatal fires, or have declined to be interviewed without legal representation or a grant of immunity, or have been ordered by their agencies not to cooperate, subverting the basic purpose of a wildfire investigation – to learn lessons that can save lives.

When nineteen members of the Granite Mountain Interagency Hotshots were killed on the Yarnell Hill Fire in 2013 – the greatest loss of life on an organized wildland fire crew in over a century – families of the those lost filed more than a dozen notices of wrongful death claims and homeowners filed over a hundred damage claims, collectively amounting to potential settlements of tens of millions of dollars. The legal situation became even more contentious when two Arizona state agencies conducted separate investigations that flatly contradicted each other. The Arizona State Forestry Division,, which was responsible for management of the fire, issued its report less than three months after the fatalities and, in an acknowledged effort to get away from the pattern of blame in previous reports, found "no indication of negligence, reckless actions, or violations of policy or protocol." That report, however, was over-hasty, made serious errors, and came in for heavy criticism. Wildland Fire Associates, an independent contractor hired by the Arizona Division of Occupational Safety and Health (ADOSH), carried out the second investigation and found "serious and willful" safety violations, directly contradicting the initial report.

ADOSH required a focus strictly on workplace safety issues, not the broader mandate of the first investigation. Even so, the findings of the two reports were so starkly opposite that they could have been written about different fires. The same conflict at the federal level, between previous fire reports and those by the Occupational Safety and Health Administration, also resulted in divergent findings, bad feelings on both sides, and worse.

In this case, ADOSH proposed fines of $559,000 against the Forestry Division. The fines were appealed; a broad settlement finally was reached that included improvements in safety practices and payments to the families. Thanks to the digital age, enormous volumes of background materials about the fire were released to the public, enlarging upon and in some cases contradicting the established picture of what had happened.

At the federal level, the Forest Service today keeps a list of managers available for assignment to investigation teams, either from the top ranks or at the regional or lower levels, depending on the severity of the event. Subject matter experts can be added as needed. Given ample time, investigation teams have produced results that stand up well to outside scrutiny. But the situation is inherently heartbreaking, the legal process enflamed, and social media ready to amplify opinion regardless of merit. The challenge to identify mistakes without being overly judgmental is no easy task. Even so, the long-term trend, from blame to learning, is perhaps the best cause for hope.

BY CONTRAST, IN 1953 when the formal investigation of the Rattlesnake Fire blamed the fire and not the people for the deaths, there was no serious challenge. The board's report does not even discuss whether the supervisors might have been negligent in failing to anticipate the violent wind shift, remarking instead that the wind change appeared to be a normal evening downdraft – which it certainly was not. The fire report specifically exonerates Lafferty, and by extension Thomas and Ewing, from the charge that they waited too long to warn the mission crew, which surely would have been a point of debate, perhaps unfairly, if the fire were to happen today. "There can be no question," the report states, "that Lafferty recognized the threat of danger promptly after the spot fire began to spread rapidly up the hill and acted in accordance with the best judgment he could formulate in the brief moment available for decision."

That brief moment, however, lasted no less than fifteen minutes.

Gleeson reported in his newspaper accounts, and others agreed, that fifteen to twenty minutes elapsed between when the spot fires started and when Lafferty took off at a run to warn the mission crew. "The forestry officials gathered around the point where I stood were so concerned at the unexpected change that they forgot about the missionaries," Gleeson told the *San Francisco Chronicle*, using more accusatory language for the out-of-town press than he had in his *Willows Journal* story for local consumption.

Today, a phrase like "forgot about the firefighters" would likely result in criminal charges.

The board of review in fact gave some thought to the subject of negligence and initially considered blaming the firefighters for their own deaths, as many a fire report has done: the dead, after all, cannot speak for themselves. An early version of the findings said, "The tragedy may have been avoided had there been another warning lookout posted. An earlier warning would have given sufficient time for escape."

Blaming victims for what befell them is a dubious business at best, and the final draft of the report does take a milder position: "The decision of Powers and Vote to eat on the Missionary Spot Fire can be interpreted in only one way. What they observed from their vantage point on the Missionary Spot Fire did not appear to present any undue danger to them or their men."

> Today, a phrase like "forgot about the firefighters" would likely result in criminal charges.

That's true enough, and merciful to the lost crew into the bargain, but it misses a chance to hammer home a lesson about posting lookouts. History, though, did not miss the point: the Rattlesnake Fire has been held up before generations of firefighters as a glaring example of the danger of failing to post a lookout.

A suspicion has abounded for years that the Forest Service deliberately "loses" old fatality reports, just as surgeons are said to bury their mistakes. The Rattlesnake Fire report is no exception. Key portions of the report relating to exact times and distances are missing from the copy kept at the Mendocino National Forest headquarters.

A search of regional archives in San Francisco turned up multiple references to the report, but no complete copy. My inquiry, however, yielded an example of how a report can be lost through simple carelessness, and not incidentally put to rest an old suspicion about a specific "lost" report. Two days after the Rattlesnake Fire in July, the Forest Service Northern Region headquarters in Missoula, Montana, mailed the "original" report for the Mann Gulch Fire to the Mendocino National Forest for use as a reference in the Rattlesnake Fire investigation. By October, officials in Missoula had become worried.

"If this report has served its purpose to you and you still have it, we would appreciate its return," wrote A.E. Spaulding, an assistant regional forester.

Spaulding's letter prompted a paper chase, which ended as these things usually do – with nobody admitting that they had seen the Mann Gulch report. "We are not only sorry – but our collective face is red for we cannot locate the Mann Gulch Report," Leon Thomas replied to Spaulding on November 17. "Apparently this original Mann Gulch report has been misfiled or lost."

Years later when my father Norman Maclean and his research partner Laird Robinson began to pull together the record of the Mann Gulch Fire for what became the book *Young Men and Fire,* they could not at first locate the fire report. "Without the report, we had no concrete foundation," Robinson said. It took a year and a half for them to run down an extra copy, fortunately tucked away in Forest Service archives.

Likewise, the Rattlesnake Fire report had been mislaid rather than buried. I interested David R. Weise, a Forest Service fire scientist in California, in the search and, using his computer and a knowledge of fire bureaucracy, he located the full Rattlesnake report in an archive of old fire documents called *Firebase,* which at the time was stored in the Forest Service R5 Regional Office library at Mare Island on San Pablo Bay, California.

Today, many of the old fire reports have become available online, greatly facilitating the understanding of fire history and preserving that history for posterity. While updating this story a decade after it was first published, I was able to locate and download the full Rattlesnake Fire report in less than a minute using an online search engine. When I did the original research for the Rattlesnake story in 2001, it took many months and numerous trips to California to do the same thing. I later obtained a report appendix, thanks to a regional Forest Service historian, with witness statements that I had gathered piecemeal laid out neatly and in full.

The complete fire report indeed has precise footage for the distances from the Missionary Spot Fire to where the firefighters' bodies were found. When I found that out in 2001, it not only defused suspicions about "buried" facts, but also raised the tempting possibility of a reconstruction of the race with fire.

The twenty-six minutes allowed in the report for the race, from about 10:15 p.m. when Lafferty started out to warn the men, until 10:41 p.m., when stopped watches show that fire overtook the crew, looks dubious at first glance. The ground is rough and steep but the distances are not great. It appears, surveying the terrain from Alder Springs Road, that men in a hurry should be able to cover the distance in far less than twenty-six minutes.

A reconstruction based on times and distances in the report could settle the question of negligence once and for all, we thought. If a rerun came in at close to twenty-six minutes, then the report was probably solid and there was no issue. If the race had been substantially shorter, however, say by fifteen minutes, then there could be a negligence issue. It would mean that the supervisors at Powderhouse Turn waited an unnecessarily long time, perhaps a half hour after first seeing the threatening spot fire in the bottom of the canyon, before alerting the missionary crew. A reconstruction would be helpful in other ways, too. Precisely locating the site of the Missionary Spot Fire should provide a better understanding of what Lafferty, Thomas, and the others had been able to see – and not see – from Powderhouse Turn. Just exactly how hidden were the crewmen from the sight of their supervisors? Conversely, locating where the missionaries had taken their last meal might provide a better understanding of why they had posted no lookouts.

In any case, hiking the routes taken by survivors and victims would be a chance to walk in their boots and better appreciate what they had endured – the simple act of staying together on that rough ground, for example, turned out to be a daunting challenge.

As I stood thinking about this, standing on Alder Springs Road in 2001 after consulting the full fire report, Powderhouse Canyon looked remarkably similar to what it was like in 1953. Despite the effects of another fire in 1988 – fire normally occurs in this kind of chaparral about every thirty years – tall brush again covered the steep slopes. Alder Springs Road had been bypassed by a constructed section of paved highway, Route 7, on the south side of Rattlesnake Ridge, leaving the old road rough and pitted as it might have been when Pattan drove along it and set his fire – perhaps it was even in better shape back then, being the main road. Beer and soda cans, shotgun shells, bullet casings and other debris lie scattered along the road. Alder Springs Road, it appears, is still a shooting gallery, far from town, just as it was for Pattan.

One visible sign of the fire is the white wooden cross, taller than a man, at Missionary Rock, the long rock knob outcropping across the canyon from Alder Springs Road. The cross is something of a mystery, or it was for many years. Anyone familiar with the fire might assume it's a memorial to the fallen of the Rattlesnake Fire, probably set there by New Tribes Mission. That is not necessarily so; a smaller wooden cross planted deep in one of the canyon's ravines is a memorial to a teenaged couple killed in more recent years when their car plunged off Alder Springs Road.

The large white cross has no inscription on it, no tablet along Alder Springs Road, nothing to explain itself. It appeared one morning in 1993 and has caused speculation ever since. Who put it up and why?

One remaining artifact of the fire is a portion of the old bulldozer line that was cut in to reach the bodies. Volunteers keep it mostly cleared from just north of Powderhouse Turn east along the ridge toward Missionary Rock. You have to look hard for it, but it's visible from across the way on Alder Springs Road. Photographs taken directly after the fire, however, show the bulldozer road extending another hundred yards or so beyond Missionary Rock, to the site where most of the bodies were found, and that section has disappeared under the creeping chaparral.

If that final section could be identified and followed, then it ought to be possible, we thought, using the precise distances in the fire report, to fix locations where the bodies were found, and to accurately reconstruct the timing of their race with fire.

This race involved the twenty-four missionaries and Ranger Powers, who were all at the spot fire, plus Lafferty, who scrambled down to warn them and was nearly caught by the fire. It proved easier than I had imagined to collect enough people to play all the firefighter roles, including those of the crewmen who were on the firelines above Alder Springs Road, far from the Missionary Spot Fire.

The Rattlesnake Fire on the Mendocino is the worst disaster for wildland firefighters in the history of northern California, and Cal Fire regards the Rattlesnake Fire as its own tragedy. A friend of mine, John R. Hawkins, was assistant chief in nearby Butte County (later named Cal Fire's Riverside unit fire chief), and long ago recognized that a re-enactment would be valuable for his agency; he had no trouble signing up thirty firefighter volunteers for our trip, several of them serious students of the Rattlesnake Fire, to re-enact the firefighters' roles.

We gathered at the foot of Powderhouse Canyon on a mild day in January. The lack of summer foliage made it easier to see the ground, easier to gauge the slope steepness – which was not the case on the July date of the fire.

The uniformed firefighters arrived in everything from sport utility vehicles to pumper engines, and we set off in a caravan up the old Alder Springs Road to Oleta Point, where Pattan had fired his .22 rifle.

The ground was littered with spent shells. Someone picked up a shell casing and tried to make a joke of it: "Hey, Pattan's shells!" But the occasion had a solemnity to it and nobody laughed.

2018 – spent .22 shells at Oleta Point

A high cutbank rises abruptly from the road at Oleta Point, but 240 feet farther on, at the ignition spot of the Rattlesnake Fire, a little gully with tufts of grass starts up from the road, a perfect funnel to help a fire take off. We divided our forces, and one group went up the little gully to trace the initial path of the fire. If they followed the fire's route correctly, they would come out at the point on the ridge top where the fire briefly slopped over Rattlesnake Ridge and started down the other side.

The rest of us, meanwhile, drove on to Powderhouse Turn and made it our headquarters, just as the firefighters had in 1953. From there we had no trouble locating the likely locations of the old firelines, though they were grown over and no longer readily visible. The first line, well marked on old maps, leads straight up from Powderhouse Turn to the aptly named High Point, on the crest of Rattlesnake Ridge. This was the line that was supposed to block the fire's advance and from which a backfire was started. The climb up was steep but short.

The second leg of fireline, built from High Point along Rattlesnake Ridge to contain the fire on its upper side, is now a two-track jeep trail and makes for easy walking. We paced distances based on the report and found the likely spot where the fire slopped over. Containing the slopover meant getting below it on rocky, steep terrain, but the fire was moving slowly downhill after cresting the ridge and there was time to catch it. Still, it would have been a tough scramble to get below the fire and do the hard work with hand tools to stop it.

We waited there for the other group to climb up from Alder Springs Road, the group tracing the fire's initial path, with the hope that they would appear right where we were standing and confirm our calculations about the location of the slopover. We waited a long time. When they finally showed, they indeed came out at our location, indicating that we likely had the right spot for the slopover. But they had scattered on the climb and showed up singly or in two and threes, a herald of difficulties to come. It's easy to lose your bearings on the rocky, brush-covered slopes, which appear to be smooth rolling hills but are raked and corrugated with countless deep ravines well hidden by chaparral.

We regrouped at Powderhouse Turn and addressed the day's main problem: the race with fire.

We decided that everyone should follow Lafferty's path from Powderhouse Turn and on to the bulldozer line, to the likely spot where he first shouted down to the mission crew, and then descend downslope toward the Missionary Spot Fire. Once there, we would again divide into two groups, one to follow the route of the nine survivors back up the side of the ridge and the other to follow the down-canyon path taken by the fifteen victims. We would track our times for each leg of the journey.

We looked out from Powderhouse Turn onto a bland winterscape, nothing like the dramatic play of lights and shadows on the night of the fire. Lafferty had taken off from the turn at a dead run along the road to the dynamite shed, then turned up onto the dozer line that had been cut across the slope that day as a firebreak. When he had gone far enough that headlamps winked up at him – the mission crew at supper – he had dropped off the dozer line and down into the chaparral trying to get close enough to be heard.

185

We followed his path. It took us each an average of a minute and a half to go from Powderhouse Turn to the bulldozer line and then make our way to the likely spot where Lafferty began to yell at the mission crew – directly upslope from the site of the Missionary Spot Fire. A few more seconds likely passed as the mission crew tried to sort out what Lafferty was yelling.

Dropping off that line into the dense chaparral, as Lafferty did, felt like stepping off the edge of the known world. The brush, even without most of its leaves, closes around you. Visibility is reduced to a few feet in every direction except straight up. The brush can be rubbery and spongy or it can scrape like cat claws on bare skin. Sometimes you bounce off the brush and have to back up and find another way through; sometimes, if a fire isn't chasing you, you crawl through the brush or even shove backward through it. When you grab a handful of the stuff for balance, it often breaks off or pulls out at the roots.

Squiggly contour lines on a topo map cannot begin to convey the intense isolation of the actual location of the Missionary Spot Fire, in a sea of chaparral on the far side of the first spur ridge down from Powderhouse Turn. From the place where the crew sat down to eat, on the low down-gulch side of the spot fire, you cannot see either up to Powderhouse Turn or down to the bottom of the canyon where a killer fire crackled to life. Of course there is also no sightline from the turn back down to the spot fire.

The site feels almost protected, in some strange way, but there are no open or obvious pathways to safe zones, no clear escape routes through the dense chaparral jungle. The failure of the crew to post lookouts while they ate was indeed a serious error and worthy of being inscribed forever after in the Ten Standard Fire Orders: "Post a lookout when there is possible danger."

At the site of the Missionary Spot Fire someone from our modern-day group picked up a rusted lid from a can, likely a food can, stamped with the numbers 4 51. The mission crew ate sandwiches and milk, not canned rations – not to say one of them didn't have a can of something in his pocket. But the numbers 4 51 suggest April 1951, in time for the fire, and the lid brought strange looks to people's faces.

The nine survivors who worked their way up toward Lafferty had a surprisingly brief scramble up the slope – at least surprisingly brief to us. They had found different paths to follow, so we tried several routes. It is flat impossible to run in the brush, at least not for more than a few steps. Well-conditioned men in our group, going hard, took from two to two and a half minutes to cover the ground from the Missionary Spot Fire back up to the old bulldozer line. It's tough going, but most of the nine survivors likely made their ascent in close to our times. Stous and Etherton, the last survivors to emerge, probably took substantially longer, because Etherton fell down and Stous had to help him along.

"I was nearly dead," Etherton said later. "I just made it. I don't know what happened to the others. They just scattered. I was wondering all the time whether each step would be my last and I would fall."

The cross at Missionary Rock in 2001

It took us about five minutes to cover the ground from the point where Lafferty began his run at Powderhouse Turn to the point where he and the nine survivors were safely back near the turn. Lafferty's run to warn the men took a minute and a half, by our reckoning. Add thirty seconds to a minute for the missionaries to pull themselves together, and then add two to two and a half minutes for their race with fire and you have roughly five minutes.

In most of those first minutes, the fifteen other men had no cause for panic. They headed down the canyon, by their own choice or trusting Lafferty, as the fire ran up the side of the canyon, chasing the nine who would survive. Powers appears to have formed the fifteen men into a line with himself at point, or at least to have taken the point – the headlamps were seen to move in single file, and later events showed that the ranger was at or near the head of the line. The brush surely helped keep them in line, because the men in front broke trail for those who followed.

Everything changed during those first five minutes: the violent wind hit Powderhouse Turn and the fire turned ninety degrees and poured downhill, turning away from the nine who barely survived and heading instead for Powers and his group of doomed firefighters.

As we left the site of the Missionary Spot Fire and began to follow the downhill route of the group that had been with Powers, we instantly discovered that there was no way they could have seen the key developments transpiring behind them – the igniting of the spot fire downslope of them, its initial upward run, and then its ninety-degree turn that set it on a path directly toward them. At the beginning of their race with fire, the spur ridge on which the Missionary Spot Fire was burning blocked their view to the rear, in the direction of Powderhouse Turn. As we took our first steps following the route Powers and the others had taken, we found ourselves heading off the spur ridge on a course for the bottom of a draw, from where we would have to start up yet another spur ridge. The farther down we went, the less we could see in *any* direction. We slid the last yards into the draw's rocky, damp bottom, which is no more than twenty inches wide.

The facing slope is steep, crumbly, sharp, and dense with chaparral. We climbed out of the draw, grabbing brush to help ourselves along. At this point in the race with fire, the flames behind the crew were growing into an inferno. We realized as we struggled upward, continuing to follow the path taken by Powers and his group, that even a towering flame wall behind us would have been invisible to the retreating firefighters. Even as we gained elevation, the spur ridge behind us blocked our view in that direction.

Once we reached the crest of the first spur ridge beyond the Missionary Spot Fire, we realized that this was the place where the men for the very first time could see the monster chasing them. What a shattering moment of terror that must have been! A colossal wave of flame crested the spur ridge to their rear, sudden, inexplicable, and horrifying: from this point on, they knew they were in a race for their lives. Someone must have shouted for them to throw down their tools, because investigators found many shovels and rakes within steps of this spot in confirmation, as if it were needed, that this was the point of their first real awareness.

They were not the only ones that night to toss away their tools, severing the link between a man and his work. David Pesonen, the young firefighter who went on to head the CDF, was assigned to patrol the area in the aftermath of the fire and pick up any tools he found. "I think I must have found fifteen Pulaskis and shovels that had been thrown over the side of the hill," he said in later years. "Thousands of dollars worth of equipment. Canteens, backpack pumps, shovels, Pulaskis, brush hooks, axes, just heaved out in the brush by crews. In fact, I still have one of those shovels."

Our present-day group looked out from this ridgeline at a sea of unbroken chaparral stretching in every direction. Every step took us farther from the safety of Powderhouse Turn. The canyon gaped ahead, seemingly without end. Alder Springs Road was an impossible distance over to our right, across the deep bottom of the canyon.

It had taken us three minutes and forty seconds to scrabble from the location of the Missionary Spot Fire to the crest of this first spur ridge, where the fifteen saw flames and threw tools. By then, Lafferty and the nine survivors had begun to trickle in to Powderhouse Turn.

Ahead, we faced another spur ridge, this one even steeper and rockier than the one we had just climbed. Missionary Rock, like a huge gray Roman nose, juts out from along the crest of this ridge, and the big white cross stands atop the Rock. As we headed for the next ridge, we descended again into another draw that blocked our view. A flying crow would have made the next ridge in a short straight line; we were forced to struggle far down before we could start up. The headlamps of the fifteen had been watched, following this roller-coaster route, and in the aftermath more tools were found scattered along this route.

As the fifteen clambered up the second spur ridge, as we were doing now, the process of natural selection began to assert itself. Two men fell behind. Two others, both fit and strong, split off on their own, figuring their chances were better alone: Stanley Vote, the foreman who sang and played accordion, hooked left and headed almost straight up for the top of Powderhouse Ridge; Hitchcock, the farm boy who sang duets with his sister, veered right and angled down toward the bottom of Powderhouse Canyon, aiming for Alder Springs Road.

Ahead of us, upward toward the white cross, there was no pathway to follow, no obvious route to mirror the final steps of the rest of the men. Even with no fire behind us, our group began to break up as we each found our separate ways to the long crest of this second ridge and to the cross on its protruding knob. You have to keep your eyes on the ground to avoid tripping. You wait in frustration for the man ahead to break through the brush. As he passes through, the brush springs back and then you too must fight your way through it while the man behind you waits his turn.

Most of the crew managed to stay with Powers, probably by following their companions' boot heels; or at least they converged around Powers at the end. Nearing Missionary Rock, at the crest of this second spur ridge, they again could see the flames coming after them. As the men neared exhaustion, the fire perversely grew stronger.

The leading edge of the fire, a shimmering wave of overheated gases, caught the last man in line just yards short of the ridge crest, at a distance of 660 feet from the Missionary Spot Fire. The fire swept on over him and caught a second straggler another 60 feet farther along, still short of Missionary Rock.

The bulk of the crew, eleven now with those two men down and Stous and Hitchcock off on their own, found flatter ground on the crest of the ridge and briefly accelerated – there is a long gap between the first two bodies and the rest. The eleven almost certainly passed over the top of Missionary Rock, about where the cross is located, because going below it, as we discovered by trying, would mean a long and arduous climb down and around a sheer rock face. The fire would have caught them there long before they could climb back up the other side.

Directly over the top of the ridge, just beyond where the cross now stands, the eleven ran into a virtual wall of brush. It's easy to see what mostly held them together from that point on: they were following trail broken by a point man. Two of the men, though, became separated from the main group, one angling slightly above and the other slightly below.

Behind them the fire leaped ravines, accelerated on upward slopes, and hurtled through the air on the downcanyon wind.

Every step now brought them closer to the lip of the next ravine, which was broader and steeper than any they had yet traversed. Their position was hopeless, and by this point they may have known it.

The fire caught the main group of nine in a sea of chaparral at a point "slightly in excess of 1,000 feet from the Missionary Spot Fire," according to the fire report, and a few dozen yards from the precipice leading into the next ravine. The two men who were separated from the others were found nearby, at distances respectively of 1,040 feet and 920 feet from the Missionary Spot Fire.

Just another 300 feet

Vote and Hitchcock made it a long way. Vote struggled almost halfway to the crest of Powderhouse

Ridge, where he would have been safe. When the fire caught him, he was 275 feet above the main group, a little more than 300 feet below the crest of the ridge, and 995 feet from the Missionary Spot Fire.[5]

Glenn "Cecil" Hitchcock made it the farthest of all, and by a wide margin. He crossed down the bottom of Powderhouse Canyon and was less than 300 feet from Alder Springs Road up the other side when his legs caught in wild grapevines or berry bushes, as his sister Mavis was told afterward. His struggle took him 1,540 feet, more than 500 yards from the Missionary Spot Fire, half again as far as anyone else.

Rumors and reports persisting to this day say the crew dug shallow foxholes at the end and died slow deaths. Hensley, the bulldozer operator who reported that the fingers of one body were broken backward – it was Vote's body – took that as proof of digging. But there are likelier explanations. Vote could have broken his fingers as he clawed his way up the ridge. Or the extreme heat, which can twist and snap even the biggest bones in the human body, could also have done it.

---

[5] Dalrymple, Tishner and Will have discussed the decision processes that resulted in the distances between the places where some of the men fell. "The crew basically went into an individual survival mode," explained Will, "once they made the ridge right above the big cross. The fire was making a run below them, and Stan went full adrenalin and busted uphill against the grain of the brush in an attempt to make it to Powderhouse Ridge. He knew there was a dozer line on top." The actual location of these decision points isn't known, of course; the three also believe that young Cecil was the first to break ranks - and make his dash for safety. "That's the only rationale we can come up with that makes any sense," said Will. "In terms of actual decision points, we really don't know. Our take is that the decision point was pure survival."

Gleeson and others reported that some of the crew managed to dig foxholes six to ten inches deep. These reports are frustrating because they never note where the holes were dug, or which men dug them, and of course there are no photos as proof. There is nothing in any official document to support the digging story, and at least one document tried to refute it. The Forest Service issued a white paper in August 1953 rebutting a lengthy list of rumors, including the report of foxholes. "All evidence on the ground indicates that it was very sudden," the paper says. "Speed and intensity of the fire was such that death was probably instantaneous."

Foxholes and fires were much on people's minds in 1953, however, which may have helped inspire the digging story. The feature film *Red Skies of Montana*, which is loosely based on the 1949 Mann Gulch Fire, had been released the year before. The movie violates true history in a finale that portrays firefighters digging foxholes to save themselves, which for certain did not happen in Mann Gulch, where just as with the Rattlesnake Fire a raging firefront caught up to and overwhelmed men moving as fast as they could to escape. That movie digging scene, however, echoed the gritty military tactics of the Korean War: the year the film came out, 1953, was the year an armistice ended three years of fighting. The renowned fire historian Stephen Pyne believes the movie scene to be a "clear parable of the Korean War," as well as part of the metaphor of fire as war.

The last yards – in 2001

Our group slowly followed the final yards of the Rattlesnake race with fire. Under the chaparral we discovered traces of the uphill edge of the old bulldozer line, from a couple of inches to a foot high, the last yards of the dozer line constructed to recover the bodies. We gave up keeping time for this leg of our journey, because we shuffled along following the edge of the cut, lost in our own thoughts and images of what had happened here. We later figured that the eleven men could have covered this ground in a minute or less. When the dozer edge gave out, we realized we had reached the end of the line.

It was a ghostly moment. The chaparral made it difficult to see people only a few feet away. Everyone except for me was a firefighter and could imagine his own end coming in a lonely spot like this one. No one thought they would have spent their last seconds digging in shale and hardpan, and we found no such depressions in the earth. But strange things do happen at the extremities of human experience.

Crosses on the slope in 2001

One of our bunch speculated on the last thoughts of the missionaries. They might have taken hope, he said, from the Bible story of the three Jews – Shadrach, Meshach, and Abed-Nego – who were cast into a fiery furnace by King Nebuchadnezzar because they'd refused to worship a golden calf. "And they walked in the heart of the flames, praising God and blessing the Lord," it says in the Book of Daniel. That story has a happy ending: impressed by their faith, the Lord intervenes and saves the men.

Whatever the missionaries were thinking, they acted as though they had a message for one another. The nine men found at this place were heaped together – there is no other way to describe it. Perhaps they huddled together to take comfort from a human touch and a common faith. Or perhaps the brush stalled Powers, who was found farthest along, probably in the lead, and the others just piled into him. They appear in photographs of the scene to be straining upward, reaching for the high ground.

But there was no protection from the fire. The men almost surely died or were struck unconscious before the flames arrived, when a huge wave of superheated gas surging invisibly ahead of the flames overtook them in a flash. The superheated gas entered their mouths and noses and seared the delicate tissues of the nose, mouth, pharynx and trachea; the tissues stiffened and ceased to carry oxygen to their lungs. The men died within seconds, and the flames came on.

We stood there thinking private thoughts until one of our party broke the silence.

"This place is sacred to the memory of those who died here," he said in a conversational manner, though his words echoed Lincoln's Gettysburg Address and were well considered. "We, by remembering them and learning from their deaths, give meaning to what happened here: that they did not die in vain; that their deaths give the gift of life to others who come after."

There was nothing to add to those words. We stood silently for a few moments, then called it a day and made our way back to Powderhouse Turn.

The time had come to pull our notes together. We had broken down the race with fire into four distinct legs:

- Leg #1 – It took us one and a half minutes to cover Lafferty's route from Powderhouse Turn to the place where he first yelled down at the mission crew. This time matched the accounts of two witnesses, Thomas and Gleeson, who said the run took Lafferty no more than a minute or two. Time elapsed: one minute thirty seconds.

- Leg #2 – We allowed thirty seconds to a minute for the crew to get up and start moving in response to Lafferty's yells, which seems reasonable considering the confusion over what Lafferty was saying. Time elapsed: one minute.

- Leg #3 – It took us two to two and a half minutes to cover the route of the nine survivors up the slope from the Missionary Spot Fire to the bulldozer line. The official report gives no time estimate for this leg of the race, but survivors said it was no more than a few minutes. Time elapsed: two minutes thirty seconds.

- Leg #4 – It took us more than eight minutes to cover the route of Powers and the fourteen missionaries from the Missionary Spot Fire to the place where nine of the bodies were found. That breaks down as seven minutes fifteen seconds for the leg to Missionary Rock and our estimate of another minute for the final hundred yards. Time elapsed: eight minutes fifteen seconds.

Added together (not including the third leg, which was separate from and simultaneous with the fourth), the total elapsed time, from the time Lafferty started out from Powderhouse Turn until flames caught Powers and the eight missionaries, was ten minutes, forty-five seconds.

Something was way off. Our time was less than half the twenty-six minutes written in the official report, which states that the supervisors noticed the spot fire at 10 p.m., Lafferty began running toward the Missionary Spot Fire at 10:15, and the deaths occurred at 10:41, the last time taken from the stopped watch of one of the missionaries. But by our calculations, if Lafferty began his run at 10:15 the end should have come about 10:25, or given a bit of leeway, no later than 10:30.

The difference of 10 to 15 minutes is striking enough to raise a red flag and should not be dismissed. At least some of the times noted in the official report had to be flat wrong. Could the report's authors have softened the blow for the fire's supervisors, excusing them from any hint of negligence, by nudging the numbers around to make it look as though their time of forgetfulness about the missionaries was shorter than it actually was? The supervisors, after all, included Ewing, who had forgotten men before and consequently lost eleven of them on the Hauser Creek Fire. It wasn't a pleasant thought; nobody in our party had a wish to make charges like that against men who were long gone and many of whom had been deeply affected by the tragedy. And because we had stood where the missionaries and Powers died, in that lonely expanse of chaparral, we knew that a few extra minutes of warning would have made no difference whatsoever to the outcome. Perhaps the time difference was a simple honest mistake: these things happen. Accuracy and integrity make a difference to the generations who follow, who try to learn life-saving lessons from reports like that one. Missionaries are not the only ones who live by faith.

The 10 p.m. start for the wind shift is a reliable time. "About 10 o'clock the wind began to come up again," the *Willows Journal's* Gleeson told fire investigators. "I am certain of this time because I had then looked at my watch. It was merely a glance and the time was either two minutes to, or two minutes after 10."

The time for the start of Lafferty's run, given as approximately 10:15 in the official report, could be off by five minutes without damage to anyone's credibility. In addition, the watches stopped at 10:41 may have been off by perhaps another five minutes or so. The report unfortunately never explains how many watches were found, where they were found, and whether they agree with one other. In an appendix to the report are photos of three watches, but they are not identified or described in any way, they do not appear to agree with one another, and there is at least one watch missing from the report. Giving the report the benefit of a couple of five-minute approximations doesn't seem an injury to truth, under these circumstances. Adding in both five-minute possibilities, then, the report's time for the race would drop from twenty-six minutes to sixteen minutes, which would bring the official version closer to our elapsed time, which can be rounded off at eleven minutes. But that still leaves a five-minute gap, and giving that away and simply calling the official report and ours a match, on top of the two previous five-minute gifts, is going too far. Our reconstruction was done with precision and our times were reliable.

The fire's supervisors and the board of review were somehow five minutes short of respectability.

I was due to arrive at the Mendocino National Forest Supervisor's Office in Willows the next morning to go over photographs of the fire and other materials with Greg Greenway, a Forest Service archaeologist, who was helping me with my research. Greenway had discovered an archive of photo negatives from the fire, including one of the fire burning, and he had sent them out to be printed. As I drove there to look over the materials with him, the words "five minutes, I need five minutes" kept ringing in my mind; I wanted those minutes to appear from somewhere and solve the mystery of the time difference in favor of the past, leaving the lessons of the past intact. As Greenway and I sorted through the photos, Rich Rushforth, a forest biologist and former Mendocino Hotshot, overheard us talking about the fire. He darted from the room and returned in minutes with a box of documents and artifacts. I had already looked through the box, but I did want to see it again. The box contained a torn manila envelope with Raymond Sherman's belongings, and I had brought along a zip lock bag as a replacement for their envelope, to keep the artifacts from spilling further.

I shook out the contents of the envelope: a few fragments of trouser and shirt fabric, the cowboy belt buckle, with figures of a bucking horse and rider, and the watch with the large initials R.S. on the wristband, which were used to identify the body. Clearly visible on the back of the watch were the words "water and shock protected." The watchmaker was obviously unfamiliar with the effects of wildfire.

The crust of shale and glass on the watch face, completely obscuring the hands, gave it more the appearance of a bracelet than an old timepiece. This watch was not included in the photo gallery with the three other watches in the official report, for the obvious reason that you couldn't read the time.

The more I looked at the watch the more curious I became. Stopped watches are a regular and rather ghostly feature of fatal wildfires, a lasting memorial to the moment when time ended for a firefighter. But this watch had been stuffed away in a paper envelope as though of no significance, and there it had lain for almost fifty years. What if it displayed a time different from the 10:41 the official report had fixed as the time of death, the time based on the other watches? What if the five minutes Lafferty and the others needed were right there under the layer of melted glass and grit on the face of Sherman's watch? The possibility was too compelling to ignore.

"Greg, would you mind if I tried to scrape this watch face clean?" I asked, adding as much to myself as to him, "I'd be tampering with a historic artifact."

Greenway answered without hesitation. "Go for it," he said. "That's why we have this stuff here, to answer questions."

I opened my pocketknife and gingerly poked at the amalgam on the watch face.  It was stuck hard. I forced in the knife tip and a big chunk of grit popped off, exposing a portion of the watch face down to bare metal. The numbers on the watch face were nearly obliterated. Surely the delicate hour and minute hands could not have survived. Neither was visible.

I stuck the knife in again, and out snapped another chunk of grit. What a disappointment! About half the watch face was now exposed, but no hands were seen. Maybe they had become embedded in the grit and I'd just snapped them off, and whatever time they had recorded was now forever lost.

At this point, I nearly gave up. What I was doing felt like waking the dead. Oddly enough, I drew inspiration at this moment from Forest Service Chief McArdle, who in 1953 had instructed the board of review on how to treat the relatives of the fifteen victims.

"Deal considerately with them and remember the depths of their sorrow," McArdle wrote in July 20 letter, directly after the fire. "Imagine yourself, for this purpose, in their position. Nevertheless, within these limits, get the facts."

Be respectful but get the facts. Advice to live by.

I drew a deep breath and stabbed again with the knifepoint. Another chunk of grit came off, and there, improbably, was a delicate steel minute hand pointing to the thirty-six-minute position, exactly five minutes before the 10:41 time reported in the official report as the final minute. Lafferty and the others had their extra five minutes.

He and the other men had reacted as quickly as could be expected under violent circumstances. No one had been negligent. By disturbing a relic, the past had been preserved.

I yelped. Greenway and Rushforth hurried over, perhaps worried about my mental state, and confirmed the hand's position at thirty-six minutes. I yammered out an explanation of why this was important, how five minutes made the difference between a suspicion of malfeasance and a simple difference over exact – perhaps overly exact – times, and their faces lit up, which was a credit to their tolerance for an enthusiast, because at this point I was too excited to make much sense.

The job was not finished. The hour hand had to be pointing to past ten to confirm the time.

I was so nervous I bent the minute hand slightly as I tucked the knifepoint under the last chip of grit and pried upward. The grit popped out, and under it appeared the short hour hand exactly where it needed to be, at just past ten. There was no mistake. Sherman's watch had stopped at 10:36.

Sherman had been with the nine men found heaped together at what became the end of the bulldozer line, the line we had followed to its conclusion. This meant the time on his watch could be compared with the time of our modern re-creation of the race with fire. The watch showing 10:41 could also have belonged to Vote or Hitchcock, who traveled farther and lasted longer. Of course, one or the other watch could have been off by a few or several minutes. But the 10:41 time had assumed a touchstone role in the official report.

With Sherman's watch added to the accounting, the race with fire could fit within the time estimate of the official report, allowing for variables. The start time of 10:15 could have been off by five minutes or more. The mission boys could have taken more than a minute to pull themselves together. The report's touchstone 10:41 time of death could be right for the watch-wearer, yet off for the group of nine, which included Sherman and his watch stopped at 10:36, along with its seemingly precious five extra minutes. But were they as precious as my (admittedly) burning imagination made them?

Why must everything fit together perfectly in a reconstruction? In fact, can we ever expect a dutiful report or later reconstruction to describe with precision an event as complex and disorderly as a race with a wildfire that confounded the professionals who watched it in real time? Do we try to make everything fit neatly because of the human need to reduce to yards and inches, minutes and hours, an event that, as McArdle said, plumbs the depths of human sorrow? The fire had fooled everyone. Ewing, the fire boss, made the same mistakes he had made on the Hauser Creek Fire, forgetting a crew and failing to anticipate a wind shift. But when he realized the danger on the Rattlesnake Fire, he put his life in jeopardy and ran toward the flames to help the survivors escape. He'd once made an enormous mistake, but he was no coward.

Thomas, familiar with wind shifts after dark, did not anticipate the strength of the wind shift on this fire. But he was the first to notice the spot fire endangering the mission crew and the first to call for action.

Lafferty forgot about the crew he had placed in harm's way, but the moment he realized the peril, he ran to warn them, and if the fire had maintained its initial course just five minutes longer, he probably would have lost his life, too.

Even Gleeson, the newspaperman, could have reminded someone sooner about the missionaries; he saw them head down to the spot fire. But as he later wrote, everyone at Powderhouse Turn was shocked and mesmerized by the sudden wind shift and the explosion of fire.

The mission crew could have done a better job of watching out for themselves.

But no one acted in bad faith, and that includes the board of review. They did not fudge numbers to protect their fellow supervisors Ewing, Lafferty, and Thomas. Sherman's watch now showed hard physical evidence supporting the conclusion that the board had reported the facts as they had them. The board's report had its deficiencies, if they can be called that: it dealt gently with the mission crew's failure to post lookouts and was soft on the fire supervisors' failure to anticipate the wind shift. But the report was by no means corrupt.

The reconstruction took us a long way, from a simple search for good numbers to a reasonable analysis of broad events. The journey was well worth the effort.

FIRE AND ASHES

THE HEAVY LOSS OF LIFE ON THE FIRE made the Forest Service take a hard look at its management of millions of acres of brushland in California and elsewhere. At an initial memorial organized forty years later, before I began my research into the fire, Dan Chisholm, Mendocino National Forest supervisor, said the forest became a pioneer in "pre-suppression planning," the use of fire and other tools to break up chaparral into more manageable units – and a model for the nation.

"You can see some of these units as you look across the canyon," he said, addressing a small crowd gathered for the new memorial. Chisholm was dedicating the new kiosk and interpretive plaque not far from the site of the fire along Route 7. It was easy to see behind him the black and brown scorch marks from prescribed fires that marked the slopes of Grindstone Canyon.

The efforts at better brushland management started the first spring after the fire, as soon as brush could be burned. A pair of young Forest Service men, dismayed by deaths of so many, took drip torches and on their own initiative ignited about a five-mile swath of brush in the canyon. No one was injured. They had been "dabbling gingerly" with deliberately set fire before that, remembered Joe Ely, the fire control officer on the Mendocino back in the 1950s who also helped fight the

Rattlesnake Fire. Ely was an honored guest at that first memorial in 1993.

"There was an undercurrent, which nobody wanted to bring out at the time, that if the Forest Service would do something about those brushlands to keep them safer we might not have had this terrible tragedy," Ely said in an oral history for the Forest Service. The burning program continued until the 1970s, when it came under legal challenge by environmental groups, who argued that it promoted non-native grasses. Today, the Forest Service burns 2,000 to 5,000 acres of chaparral each year on the Mendocino National Forest on a rotational schedule. Most of the burning is done by helitorch, dropping gobs of flaming gasoline gel – napalm – from helicopters.

Ely took inspiration, as well as a haunting sadness, from his experience on the Rattlesnake Fire, which he thought could have been stopped early and without fatal consequences if airplanes had been able to drop water on it. He is credited with launching one of the first efforts at aerial firefighting, a milestone accomplishment that adds greatly to the legacy of the Rattlesnake Fire. Two years after the fire, in 1955 Ely asked a pilot stationed in Willows whether he could adapt his crop-dusting airplane to drop water on a fire. Up to that time, there had been minor and unsuccessful attempts to extinguish fires from the air by dropping water-filled barrels, metal bombs, and even balloons. In a test called "Operation Firestop" in 1954 at the Camp Pendleton Marine Corps Base, a Navy Grumman TBF Avenger accomplished a free-fall water drop, soaking 250 feet of runway. The Aerial Fire Depot in Missoula, home to the Missoula

Smokejumpers, to this day has a fragmented 500-pound bomb sitting on the lawn, which causes curious stares by visitors until it is explained that the bomb was used in an early aerial firefighting experiment.

In 1955, at Ely's urging, a crop-duster pilot named Vance Nolta constructed a gate, a dump valve, and a mechanism to operate them from the cockpit of a Stearman 75 Kaydet, and with Ely looking on he tested the contraption on a grass fire deliberately started alongside the runway at the Willows airport. It worked.

In an article Ely wrote for the *Journal of Forest History* in April 1983, he credited the spirit of the crop-dusters for making the experiment possible. "Ag pilots were the last of the silk scarf and leather helmet boys. They would try anything that was exciting."

What is said to be the first drop on a live fire happened August 13, 1955, when the Stearman, again piloted by Nolta, dumped six loads of water on a log truck that had crashed and started a fire near Covelo on the Mendocino National Forest.

Then, using federal funds, six more planes were converted for the next fire season in 1956, and fighting fire from the air soon became a widespread practice. Today, it remains an essential element of firefighting.

Ely in 1957 received a $100 award from the Forest Service for his efforts; he spent it buying drinks for crop-duster pilots at a celebratory gathering. After he retired he moved from Willows to Chico and taught range management courses at California State University and at Butte College. He died in March 2006 at the age of 94.

The 1993 Rattlesnake memorial dedication turned into a family reunion for about twenty-five relatives of Ranger Robert Powers. His brother Don, a retired judge from Oklahoma City, addressed the crowd and acted as family spokesman. "My brother Bob was a student and a scholar and he was certainly an adventurer," Don Powers said. "He was challenged by God's creation. And most of all he loved people."

Bob was also a bit of a showman, according to his brother. Before leaving for the Pacific, Bob talked the pilot of the B-24 on which he served as navigator into buzzing his hometown of Salinas, Kansas. The giant aircraft flew over the town at just five hundred feet, an event said to be remembered there to this day.

After the ceremony, some drove down the old road for a look at the fire site. They invited Homer Hancock to join them, but he asked to be excused. Hancock had time and again told his story of watching the vanishing lights of the fifteen men, but he had seen enough of the Rattlesnake Fire site to last his lifetime. He held no bitterness, though. He had summed up his feelings about what happened in a statement for the Forest Service directly after the fire. "Those of us mission fellows who remain have no ill feelings in our heart because of this, knowing these things rest in the hands of Him who made us and in whom these boys loved."

Some people grumbled that there should be a marker at the actual site of the fire. Sharing this view was Don Will, superintendent of the Mendocino Hotshots, who had helped build the memorial along Route 7, a ridge over from the fire site. Powderhouse Canyon cried out for a cross, Will figured, but erecting a Christian symbol on federal land would be a legal minefield.

He gathered the Mendocino Hotshots and told them his plan. They located a couple of construction ties and went to work on them at night in a trailer. One evening they assembled at a local watering hole, the Timberline Bar and Grill in Stonyford, not far from their station and south of Powderhouse Canyon. The hotshots fortified themselves for the task ahead.

It was no small job to lug a ten-foot-high cross, a rock pry bar, a posthole digger, and other gear into Powderhouse Canyon in the dark, but the hotshots managed. Fittingly, they wore headlamps, as had the mission crew in 1953.

The hotshots located a crack in Missionary Rock and said a firefighters' prayer. Then they put their hands on the pry bar and slammed it down. When the hole was about two feet deep, they dropped in a can of snuff, some pocket change, and other little treasures, ordinary objects with special meaning, the sort of things that show up at the Vietnam Veterans Memorial in Washington, DC, known as the wall that heals. Little treasures are found at the markers on Storm King Mountain in Colorado, at the Granite Mountain Interagency Hotshots memorial site in Prescott, Arizona, and at other landmarks to those who lost their lives in service. The Mendocino Hotshots set the cross, departed, and for years after kept silent about their mission.

After this story was first published, the Mendocino Hotshots and other Forest Service personnel at the Mendocino National Forest Supervisor's Office decided

213

the time had come to build a full-scale memorial at the actual site of the fire. They set out to identify and clear out the old overgrown firelines, erect individual crosses where each of the fifteen men had fallen, construct an overlook and interpretive display, and retain and explain the wooden cross at Missionary Rock.

Volunteers joined in from local fire departments and elsewhere; construction firms and other commercial interests donated supplies.

The old bell that had called the missionaries to the fire at Fouts Springs was discovered rusting away on a farm. The owner donated the bell, and once it was cleaned and restored it was placed at the interpretive site.

The final result cost thousands of volunteer hours and several tons of donated construction materials – and very little cash.

The new memorial was dedicated at a ceremony on July 9, 2005, and it was attended by more than 300 people, including relatives of the fallen from as far away as Ecuador.

One survivor made the trip: Duane Stous, 79. He addressed the attendees at the site and, after saying he was not an emotional person, began to tell the story of what had happened that day. But when he spoke of seeing the burned bodies of the missionaries for the first time, his voice slowed; it cracked a bit and then he stopped speaking altogether. His daughter Juanita, sitting in the front row, broke into tears. "It brought back a lot of memories," Stous said later.

I had the difficult job of speaking after Stous. I said the Rattlesnake Fire was a story not just about fire, but also about community and challenges to faith and redemption by faith.

"I think the story is very important to us as people. You will never look at this canyon again the same way. It's not just brush; it's a place where wonderful and terrible things happened."

THE RATTLESNAKE SITE IS NO LONGER a lonely, trash-littered place, visited mainly as a target range. In the new century, it has become a destination site, hosting staff rides for hundreds of firefighters each year and educational or interpretive tours for others, from relatives of those who died there to the simply curious tourists. For viewing and walking, it's one of the easiest of the major fatal wildfire sites in the country.

Daren Dalrymple, a former Mendocino Hotshot superintendent, estimated that 300 to 500 firefighters each year participate in Rattlesnake Fire staff rides, an exercise taken from the military, assuming the roles of the men who fought the fire, hiking the firelines and trying to imagine the conditions they faced. On the staff rides, firefighters are challenged to go beyond the question of what happened that day to deeper questions of leadership and how to make decisions.

"I think the Rattlesnake Fire has affected the lives of a lot of young firefighters," Dalrymple said. "Hopefully they come out of it with a better understanding of fire situations, and an awareness that they are learning from what history has taught us."

At the time of the sixtieth anniversary in 2013, Dalrymple had left the hotshots for work as a fire and fuels planner for the Mendocino National Forest. Jon Tishner later served as hotshot superintendent, and both men planned to be at the site on July 9, the anniversary date. But fire proved once again, if it needed proving, that it does not care for human plans. Just before the anniversary date, Tishner and the Mendocino Hotshots were assigned to a fire in Alaska, and the night before the anniversary Dalrymple was dispatched to the Kyburz Fire on the El Dorado National Forest in northern California. That fire was held to under 600 acres. No one was injured.

One who did make it to the site for the sixtieth anniversary was Kathy Leonetti. At the time of the fire, Kathy was living at the Fouts Springs missionary camp with her parents, Allan and Roberta Boddy, and two older sisters, Alonda and Becky. In 1953 they had arrived at the camp only a week earlier after a rousing sendoff from their home church in Vancouver, British Columbia. When the big camp bell rang, the one now at the memorial site, Allan Boddy was one of those who answered the call. As he climbed onto the truck headed for the fire, he called out to his wife, "Bertie, I forgot my New Testament!" and she ran back to the little cabin where they lived and fetched it for him.

After Boddy was killed on the fire, friends helped the family get established in Portland, Oregon, where Boddy's widow Roberta spent the next twelve years completing a college education, one night school credit at a time, and working part-time to support her little family. Fortunately, Boddy had taken out a life insurance policy that enabled the family to buy a house and helped support them through lean years.

As Kathy grew up, her father was always "the elephant in the living room," a heavy but untouchable presence, forever out of reach. Roberta never talked to her children about their father; the memories of their few days as missionaries and his violent death were simply too painful. So Kathy invented imaginary fathers, one after another, until one day her older sister Alonda blurted out, "Kathy doesn't believe Dad is dead!"

Roberta replied, "Oh, of course Kathy understands that Dad is dead." For Kathy, Allan Boddy became dead from that day forward, until many years later when his memory resurrected itself in their lives. When the last of Kathy's grandparents died in the 1980s, she received in the mail a collection of news clippings about the Rattlesnake Fire – and the loss of her father and the fourteen others.

"It was the first time I knew what had happened," Kathy told me. Matters rested there for more than a decade, until in 2010 her sister Becky called her at work one day and told her to look up the Rattlesnake Fire online. By then, the internet had amassed plenty of material about the fire, including reports about the new memorial, far more and fresher information than Kathy had gleaned from the inherited collection of press clippings. "It was a shocking experience," Kathy said. And, she told herself, *I want to go.*

So in February 2010 she and her husband Frank started the eight-hour-plus drive from their home in

Oregon to the site of the Rattlesnake Fire. When they reached Willows they phoned the supervisor's office of the Mendocino National Forest and asked for directions to the site. Instead, they acquired two eager tour guides, the former and current hotshot superintendents Dalrymple and Tishner, who volunteered to take them to the site and show them around. "I knew there had to be people like her out there," Dalrymple said. "It was the best day on the hill I've ever had."

Kathy spent a bittersweet day walking where her father had walked, seeing what he had seen, and visiting the spot where his life on earth had come to an end. Eventually, she would attend the sixtieth anniversary events and bring her own children and grandchildren to the site to share the experience and pass on the legacy to a new generation. "I hadn't really understood the impact of the fire," she said. "It was the first time my dad was real to me, the first time I grieved for him. It was like finding your father and losing him at the same time."

The email below was sent from John Devino to Mendocino Superintendent Jon Tishner in January 2007.

Hello Jon,

In 1953 I was a member of a SCARWAF[6] Army unit stationed at Beale AFB. What we were basically trained for was to build and defend Air Bases for the Air Force. We also helped out during a flood in the Marysville CA area (which for some reason I missed out on).

Devino (front center) and the Army mop-up crew

All I can remember about the fire is this: At Beale AFB we were told to pack our field gear; they loaded us on trucks and, not knowing where we were going, we ended up at Mendocino.

The rangers gave us each a hand tool and a 5-minute course on how to use them. They picked about 10

---

[6] Special Category Army Redesign with Air Force

of us, and took us to a ravine (or a small canyon – I'm a city boy) and told us to spread out up the ravine. If any burning trees fell from one side of the ravine, our job was to put out any fire so it wouldn't spread to the other side. No problems at all.

RATTLESNAKE FIRE 1953
RANGER GUARD SHACK
(AFTER STEAK BREAKFAST)

Steak dinner aftermath at the Guard Station.

The exciting part was after the fire; our troops left "BUT" they forgot about us guys in the ravine. The next day when they discovered us missing, they phoned the Forest rangers, who in turn picked us up. We were tired and hungry, and the rangers took us back to their camp and cooked us each a great big steak.

Didn't know anything about men losing their lives until I was given a newspaper article. Would you like me to mail you the original article?

Sorry, that's all I can remember.
Please "Not a Hero"

John Devino

AFTER THIS STORY WAS FIRST PUBLISHED IN 2003 in the book *Fire and Ashes,* I sent a copy to Stanford Pattan. When we next talked by phone, he was defiant and upset. He repeated several times that he wouldn't have any trouble selling his paintings in the future because the book added to his public persona, but that was mostly bluster. He acknowledged that I had given him a chance to tell his side of the story, but it didn't make him happy.

Even so, we stayed in touch and over time his upset subsided. He subsequently did several paintings for me, including the painting of King Salmon. "I've developed a considerable fondness for the salmon painting," I wrote in my last letter to him in March 2004. "It reminds me – and I mean this as a compliment – of some colonial-period American art that portrays rural life using plain, primary colors."

Pattan never answered that letter, and I eventually learned that he had moved to a motel near Willows, and had become ill and stopped seeing friends. Finally, I ran across a brief death notice from the Social Security Administration, which used to maintain an online death index: *Stanford Philip Pattan, born November 15, 1926, a resident of Willows, California, died at the age of 82 on January 2, 2009.* I've never found another notice or an obituary or a news story about the death of the man who set the Rattlesnake Fire.

SEEKING OTHER TRAINING VENUES, the New Tribes Mission left Fouts Springs in stages, beginning a few years after the fire. In 1959, the camp was turned into the Fouts Springs Youth Facility, in a state program for delinquent boys, completing a moral cycle of sorts – from a shady resort during Prohibition to a place of faith under New Tribes oversight to one promising a chance of a new start for wayward young people. In August 2001 another fire, the Trough Fire, burned 25,000 acres around the youth camp, a collection of cinderblock buildings capable of housing 120 young men. Brian Cooley, the youth camp superintendent, was in his office when he looked out the window and saw a plume of smoke from the fire – later declared started under suspicious circumstances.

The flames blew off to the east and down the mountains. The following afternoon, the fire turned on a wind shift and came back uphill toward the youth camp, the reverse of the Rattlesnake Fire and its awful switch from uphill to downhill.

By the time the Trough Fire reached the camp at Fouts Springs, crews had cleared the camp's perimeter of brush, trees, and other flammable material – with three notable exceptions. When the missionaries left Fouts Springs, their cabins had remained. Over the years missionaries and their families made return visits, Cooley said, fondly poking around their old living quarters. At the time of the Trough Fire, three mission cabins still stood along the edge of the youth camp. The fire turned every one to ashes.

The youth correctional facility closed in July 2011.

New Tribes Mission confounded predictions that it would soon wither away under the hard blow of the

Rattlesnake Fire. Instead, it grew from six hundred members in 1953 to well over three thousand missionaries, in twenty countries. The current spacious headquarters in Sanford, Florida, is yet another place with a shady past that the group took on: built as the Hotel Forrest Lake in the 1920s, named for its founder, it was a favorite winter haunt of the gangster Al Capone.

FROM THE FARAWAY LOOKOUT OF HINDSIGHT, it's clear that the great tragedy fires smolder for generations, long after they've burned out on the ground. The embers of remembrance, tamped down by time but not extinguished, glimmer deep in the lives of those who carry on, until something occurs to fan them back to vibrant life. Then a kind of resurrection can take place, as happened with the Rattlesnake Fire. In this case, the fire-starter himself helped begin the process of rediscovery by breaking his decades of silence and offering an explanation, however unsatisfactory, for how it all started. Families came together and reunited with their roots: a father was found and put to rest, the lost were mourned and the dead honored. The wildland fire community, a family itself, recovered its past, revitalized old safety lessons, discovered new ones, and still pass along the legacy to a new generation: go walk where they walked, and consider well what happened here.

PASSING IT ON

O N THE FINAL DAY OF THE PHOTO SHOOT for this book, with Kari Greer on one side of the camera and Daren Dalrymple on the other side, an unexpected meet-up occurred.

Dalrymple with Gonzalez and Hartrum at Powderhouse Turn

"When Daren and I were up there," said Kari, "these two guys drove up and chatted with us briefly when we were shooting near the Gillaspy ranch. They said they were headed for the Rattlesnake site and they proceeded on to the Overlook. They must have stopped there, paid respects and read about the fire, and then walked around a bit from there."

She said the two continued all the way up to Powderhouse Turn, while she and Daren stayed at the

Overlook wrapping up the photo shoot. They watched as the hikers made their way along the stand trails and the staff ride locations, spotting them now and then through the brush and across the canyon on the north slope.

"It was interesting to see it to scale," said Kari, "the size of the guys hiking in the chaparral and their pace as they traversed the landscape. They did the entire thing, even going down to Cecil Hitchcock's cross at the bottom and clear up to Stanley Vote's cross at the top. They cross-countried up to the ridge where the dozer line had been at the time. This showed us that they knew the history and were doing the full experience.

"Daren and I made our way up to Powderhouse Turn, and we caught up with them as they were hiking out, coming up the Access Route that goes downhill to the Missionary Spot Fire. We talked a bit more with the two of them and learned that José Gonzalez was here being mentored by Daniel Hartrum, who is a former firefighter, now a teacher. José was working hard; he was wearing a Pack Test Vest and carrying a tool. They told us he was hoping to get hired onto a crew and Daniel was giving him some field experience at the site."

What a stroke of serendipity for the two of them, running onto not only Kari Greer shooting photos for this book, but also Daren Dalrymple, one of the keepers of the Rattlesnake flame.

Daniel Hartrum and José Gonzalez

Gonzalez, Dalrymple, and Hartrum at Powderhouse Turn, April 2018

Hartrum and Gonzalez hiking the slope · Guide to the trail access at the site

Two eagles on the way up to the fire site

PHOTO GALLERY

Wildland fire photographer Kari Greer took the newer photos for this book, which are the most numerous, during two trips to the site and the surrounding area in the spring of 2018. While there she drew on the generous support of three former superintendents of the Mendocino Hotshots – Jon Tishner, Don Will, and Daren Dalrymple – who are mentioned throughout this book. They contributed their long experience and deep knowledge to help understand the events of the fire and its aftermath, in which they have been key participants. Their contributions are extensive and greatly appreciated. The old photos used in this book are from the author's collection, including images taken by him, plus photos from USFS files and from other sources.

Jon Tishner, Don Will, and Daren Dalrymple

View of the Fouts Springs site

Old cabin at Fouts Springs

Escape route through the thick chaparral

Daren Dalrymple, former Mendocino superintendent, at the site of
the hotshot cross on Missionary Rock, spring 2018.

Keepers of the Rattlesnake:
Tishner, Will, and Dalrymple

Shovels on the wall of an old
building at Fouts Springs

Origin of the 1953 Chrome Fire — this line of scrub oak was noted on a
hand-drawn map of the fire. Pattan lit the fire before he lit the Rattlesnake Fire.

Fouts Springs camp in 1953 was managed by families of the New Tribes Mission.

One of the first residents of the missionary camp killed a big rattlesnake down by
the creek. The site was later home to a youth correctional facility.

233

Rock gate entrance to Fouts Springs

Nancy's Airport Café at the western edge of Willows

The old bridge over Stony Creek, just north of the town of Elk Creek

Spring turkeys at the Gillaspy ranch

A small and tight-knit little village in 1953, Elk Creek today is not much different.
With a population of maybe 160, the town's named for the creek
that runs down from the Coast Range into Stony Creek.

Dalrymple, Will, and Tishner at the memorial overlook on old Alder Springs Road

Mendocino Hotshots cross in 2018

The Alder Springs creekbed

Negotiating the chaparral brush, even with a walking stick, even in top physical shape, even in daylight, is a challenge. And then there's the poison oak.

Daren Dalrymple and Jon Tishner (Don Will in background)
take a break at Cecil's cross.

Tishner shows the angle of the "hose escape" up the
log chute below Alder Springs Road

The overlook above the fire site — memorial established on old Alder Springs Road.
Aerial overview of canyon, looking east from High Point.

Powderhouse Ridge at left, Gillsapy Ranch at canyon bottom.

Don, Jon, and Daren — plus Don's heeler Reggie — at Cecil's cross

Namesake mascot on the last day of the photo shoot

Rattlesnake rattlesnake

Resident turkey vulture (TV) near the Gillaspy ranch

Springtime attitude, on the Gillaspy ranch

Smoke on the Rattlesnake Fire — NIFC archives photo

LONG ROAD TO THE MEMORIAL

Jim Barry

THE RATTLESNAKE MEMORIAL SITE, at the overlook in Powderhouse Canyon, was a long time in coming.

For many years, the dark-of-the-night insertion of the big white cross stood as the lone marker in the canyon for the fallen of the Rattlesnake Fire, an unexplained testimonial to a fading memory. But tragedy runs deep in the human soul and has a way of coming back to life.

When Jim Barry started work for the Mendocino National Forest in 1978 he often drove past the site of the Rattlesnake Fire, because the new road to the south was under construction.

"Somebody pointed out it was the Rattlesnake Fire site, but nobody knew where they had died or much else about the site," he said. A few years later he took up a post for the Forest Service in Stonyford, not far south of the site, and when he opened a drawer in the desk he took over, he found items including an old clipping from the *Willows Journal*, with a photo of the Rattlesnake Fire victims where they had been found after the fire. The photo was one of those that had been shown to Pattan to break him down and obtain a confession. Publication of the graphic photo had caused an outcry at the time, but someone in the Forest Service had cut it out and tucked it away. "There was a little caption about them perishing on the fire," said Barry, "and I saved it. I didn't know that more than two decades later it would help me find the positions for the crosses."

Barry kept running into more links to the fire. He lived in those days on French Street in Willows with his wife, Teri, and five children, and one time a "gentleman who lived down the street" invited Barry into his house, showed him paintings he'd done, and said he'd been an outdoor guide for many years. "I didn't realize at the time that he was the arsonist," Barry said. "I went back home and told my wife, that guy's strange. Let's watch out for the children. Little things like that kept popping up in my career." While driving around the district on another occasion, Barry saw a big bell hanging over the gate entrance to a new house, and later saw it lying elsewhere in a field, almost as if it were offered for another purpose. Somebody told him the bell had come from Fouts Springs and had been rung to call the missionaries to the fire.

Years later, around the turn of the century, Barry was on a fire assignment near Storm King Mountain in Colorado, where the South Canyon Fire took the lives of fourteen firefighters in 1994. He decided to drive over to visit the South Canyon site. "I went there and saw the displays, the markers – and the light just went on."

He returned home determined to create a similar memorial for the Rattlesnake Fire, and quickly won a go-ahead from receptive Forest Service superiors. Barry and other volunteers, many from the Mendocino Hotshots, set out to reconstruct the firelines, identify the sites where the men had fallen, and place markers and crosses. They decided to retain and explain the big white cross at Missionary Rock, and planned to build a memorial at an appropriate place with a clear view of the events of the fire. But where exactly were these places? Except for the big cross, the canyon was overgrown and the old sites unmarked.

Using the original fire report and other photo evidence, they uncovered old firelines and other features. As volunteers began to brush them out, the Mendocino Hotshot superintendent at the time, Daren Dalrymple, marked the sites with stakes. Barry took the faded clipping from the *Willows Journal* that he had saved for decades, and with the photo of the precise location of the bodies he compared it with what he could see as he stood in the vicinity of where the photographer had been. "Holy cow! Man, did we hit this!" he thought. The photo was from virtually the same perspective as the spot where Barry was standing, so close that he thought the photo might actually have been taken from exactly the same place. "This was weird. Am I being guided here?" Barry wondered. "There's a rock there in that photo in the vicinity of the bodies. Just a small rock sticking out of the ground, visible in the photo. And there it was, in the same location. The rock in the hillside was the same as the rock in the picture. It didn't appear to be disturbed. That was our marker."

When this story was first published in 2003, it added to the growing enthusiasm for the memorial project. "It motivated us more to get this done," Barry said.

Volunteers joined in from local fire departments and elsewhere; construction firms and other commercial interests donated supplies. "The Glenn County Fire Chiefs Association were very supportive of the project," said Barry, "which involved all the local fire departments in the county."

The owners of the old bell donated it to the Forest Service, and willing hands cleaned and restored it and installed it at the memorial site along the old Alder Springs Road. The site they'd chosen there, though, was so narrow that Barry, who oversaw road maintenance for the Grindstone Ranger District, ordered dirt hauled in to extend it into the canyon, until it was large enough to serve as a platform for the memorial. The project took thousands of volunteer hours, tons of donated construction materials, donated labor by Cal Fire inmate hand crews – and almost no cash. The new memorial was dedicated at a ceremony on July 9, 2005, and was attended by more than 300 people, including relatives of the fallen from as far away as Ecuador.

"I put a lot of my soul into making the whole thing happen," said Barry. "I had a lot of sleepless nights reliving what I imagined they went through on the night they perished. For me, it was one of my best efforts, if not the very best. So many people have gone through the training up there now, and we hope the lessons learned have saved lives."

ABOUT THE PHOTOGRAPHER

Kari Greer

For more than 20 years Kari Greer has been photographing wildland fires and the people who wage the annual wars of summer.

She studied photography at CSU Sacramento and worked summers as a firefighter. After she graduated, it seemed a natural fit to combine fires and photography. "The bug bit, and I developed a kind of passion for it."

Greer has worked photo contracts with NIFC since the late 1990s, and has unusual access to fires and aircraft and personnel – she's earned a long-standing trust level with fire crews and management teams.

The Idaho native is a red-carded firefighter; the tools in her red bag are mostly cameras, with lenses and other associated equipment.

In February 2018 at the University of Idaho's Prichard Art Gallery in Moscow, a collection of her work was celebrated in an exhibit, "Facing the Inferno, the Wildfire Photography of Kari Greer." The exhibit was later shown in Missoula at the Fire Continuum Conference hosted by the International Association of Wildland Fire and the Association for Fire Ecology.

POV from the modern fire break